Beginner's Guide to Woodworking

CW00369927

Beginner's Guides are available on the following subjects:

Audio
Tape Recording
Radio
Television
Colour Television
Electronics
Digital Electronics
Transistors
Integrated Circuits
Computers
Basic Building Work
Electric Wiring
Domestic Plumbing
Central Heating
Woodworking
Home Energy Saving
Gemmology

Beginner's Guide to Woodworking

**Frank Underwood
and Gordon Warr**

Newnes Technical Books

The Butterworth Group

United Kingdom	**Butterworth & Co (Publishers) Ltd** London: 88 Kingsway, WC2B 6AB
Australia	**Butterworths Pty Ltd** Sydney: 586 Pacific Highway, Chatswood, NSW 2067 Also at Melbourne, Brisbane, Adelaide and Perth
Canada	**Butterworth & Co (Canada) Ltd** Toronto: 2265 Midland Avenue, Scarborough, Ontario M1P 4S1
New Zealand	**Butterworths of New Zealand Ltd** Wellington: T & W Young Building, 77—85 Customhouse Quay, 1, CPO Box 472
South Africa	**Butterworth & Co (South Africa) (Pty) Ltd** Durban: 152—154 Gale Street
USA	**Butterworth (Publishers) Inc** Boston: 10 Tower Office Park, Woburn, Mass. 01801

First published 1979 by Newnes Technical Books,
a Butterworth imprint
Reprinted 1980

British Library Cataloguing in Publication Data

Underwood, Frank
  Beginner's guide to woodworking.
  1. Woodwork — Amateurs' manuals
  I. Title II. Warr, Gordon
  684'.08   TT185   78-40596

  ISBN 0 408 00382 0

Typeset by Butterworths Litho Preparation
Department

Printed in England by Fakenham Press Ltd,
Fakenham, Norfolk

Preface

Timber is the most abundant natural structural resource available to mankind. It is also the most versatile. Timber occurs in many degrees of strength, colour and visual appearance — often of striking aesthetic value. It is easy to produce, prepare for use and work.

Over many centuries the ability to work with wood has developed with the various civilisations, and a remarkable aptitude for using woodworking tools is latent in many people from all social levels. Woodworking is a pleasant occupation; the raw materials are clean, usually fragrant, and respond readily to the tools used.

Those are some of the reasons why working with wood is a perfect hobby for anyone, a satisfying occupation and a money-saving recreation when applied to home furnishing and home maintenance. So, we present this, our guide to woodworking: by no means a complete treatise on the subject but a series of stepping stones which will guide the novice along the road to a successful participation in this most interesting of all practical crafts.

We will start by introducing the material itself, the terms used when discussing it, some of the many fixings and fittings used in constructional woodwork, and the more common terms related to woodworking. One introduction will lead to another, increasing the general understanding of the materials and the tools; then we will discuss the basic processes and practices established by many generations of trial and error, and by scientific research.

Frank Underwood
Gordon Warr

Contents

1 Introduction

Woodworking has so many facets to it that even dedicated craftsmen continue to learn about it throughout their lives. However, even acknowledged experts in any field of human activity have to start somewhere and this book is for those whose background to the craft is limited, and who are quite willing to call themselves beginners. Before we can use a material or handle tools competently we should learn something about them. Let us start with wood.

Wood

A cross section of a tree trunk, showing main parts only, is given in *Figure 1.1*. The best quality timber is cut from the heartwood (duramen); this is usually darker in colour than the sapwood, which contains living cells and is not so dense. Heartwood gives strength and support to the tree while new growth builds up around the sapwood, from the cambium layer beneath, and protected by, the bark.

Annual rings (growth rings) are formed each year: in the spring when sap is rising, and in the autumn when it is falling. Hence the names, spring wood and summer wood. The age of a tree can be calculated by counting the growth rings. Close annual rings indicate slow growth, wide ones indicate quick growth.

Growth rings of hardwoods are generally much closer than those of softwoods, and often less pronounced. Timber with close rings is usually more stable and less liable to distortion than wide ringed timber. Less than six rings to the inch in softwoods is often unacceptable for structural work.

Trees are divided into two classes: (1) broadleaf trees usually shed their leaves in winter, although some are evergreen. Such

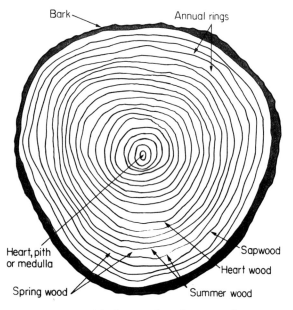

Figure 1.1. Cross section of a tree trunk

trees produce hardwood. Class (2) are the conifers, usually evergreen with needle-like leaves amongst which are produced cones. These are the softwoods.

The terms softwood and hardwood are rather inclined to be misnomers because balsa, the softest wood known and used for modelling, buoyancy aids, some stage furniture (such as a chair broken over the hero's head) etc., is classified as a hardwood while yew, once used to make longbows and now used for fencing, furniture and decorative items, is dense, hard, and very durable; although it is a softwood. A point to observe in these classifications is that softwood and hardwood are each one word. When the term soft wood (two words) is used, it indicates a characteristic of the particular species, not its classification.

Despite the reservations above, here are some general characteristics of hardwoods and softwoods.

Hardwoods	*Softwoods*
Tend to be harder and denser than softwoods	Tend to be softer and lighter than hardwoods
Slow growing, therefore annual rings tend to be close	Faster growing, therefore annual rings well spaced
Annual rings often indistinct	Annual rings usually well pronounced
Not much resin content	Some species very resinous
Knots can be very large but usually not many of them	Many small knots are common and some large ones
Wide colour range over the hardwood species, with many rich, colourful and dark shades	Mostly pale creamy white to light brown, with the exception of yew

Newly felled timber is taken to the saw mill for conversion, as the initial sawing of the round log into plank and board form is called. The most common method of conversion is 'slab' sawing, also known as slash sawing or sawing through-and-through (*Figure 1.2*). The method of sawing and the part of the trunk sawn has some influence on the timber produced as shrinkage during drying or seasoning takes place. The illustration shows a plain sawn log, which is the easiest and cheapest method of converting. Plank (*a*) would distort by cupping away from the heart side, as would plank (*c*).

Plank (*b*), referred to as a radial plank, would shrink in width but would remain fairly flat.

Planks sawn so that the growth rings meet the face at an angle of not less than 45 degrees are called quarter sawn, the most desirable timber for first class constructional work. When

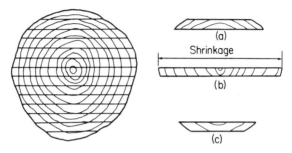

Figure 1.2. Timber conversion. Tangential planks are shown in section at (a) and (c). A radial plank is shown at (b)

the growth rings are at an angle of less than 45 degrees the plank is described as plain sawn. These planks show the fine contour-line oval grain configurations. Plain sawing can therefore produce both types.

Before timber can be used for constructional purposes it has to be dried, or seasoned, to reduce the amount of moisture in the timber (moisture content) to suit the situation where the timber will be used. There are two methods of seasoning.

Natural seasoning

Here the sawn timber is stacked on level ground with spacers or 'stickers' between the planks, to allow a free circulation of air. This is the old way, but it is slow, taking about one year for each 25 mm (1 in) of thickness of material (*Figure 1.3*). Ends of slabs may be painted or otherwise sealed to prevent too rapid drying and weights may be placed on top of the stack to prevent movement.

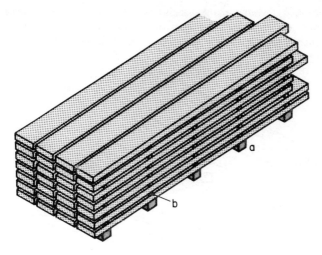

Figure 1.3. Timber 'in-stick', for seasoning

Kiln drying

This is much quicker and a lower moisure content can be achieved by the carefully controlled conditions it is possible to create in the kiln. The stacking system is similar to that used in natural seasoning. This takes place in an enclosed chamber and by a combination of steam, dry air and fans the time of drying is reduced from years to weeks.

Often timber bought at a local merchant's yard is only partially seasoned. This can lead to complications, especially with regard to shrinkage. Ideally, the timber should be carefully stacked, as for seasoning, in the place it will be used so that the moisture content can adjust to the environment. As stated earlier, timber shrinks unequally: lengthways, with the grain, nil; with the annual rings (circumferentially) considerably; across the annual rings (radially) about half as much. Poor or inefficient seasoning can lead to splitting, warping, bowing and cupping. Leaning planks against a wall, ladderlike, for long times in sun, wind or rain can also cause bowing and warping, which is practically impossible to rectify (*Figure 1.4*).

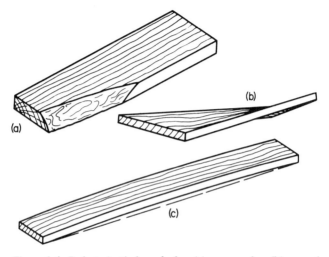

Figure 1.4. Defects in timber planks: (a) waney edge, (b) warped board, (c) bowing

Board (*b*) is twisted and (*c*) is bowed. A part waney edge is shown at (*a*). Waney edge is the outer part of the trunk covered, with bark. Some boards are sold with the waney edge for special use, such as cladding walls, but waney edges are not desirable on finished timber for structural use.

Terms

Already we have used terms which may be unfamiliar. Some of them are illustrated by the drawings but the following simple glossary will introduce a few more. It is good sense to learn the language of woodworking; you will then know what your supplier is talking about and, very importantly, he will know what you mean.

Air-dried	Seasoned as previously described, in open air conditions. Such timber will have a relatively high moisture content at least equal to the ambient climatic humidity. If used indoors and especially in heated rooms, such timber may shrink or deform unless carefully used. Generally such timber is satisfactory for normal constructional use such as roofing timbers, but during long periods of damp weather air-dried timber, and indeed any timber stored under normal climatic conditions during such periods, will have a high moisture content.
Board	Converted timber around 51 mm (2 in) or greater thickness. Manufactured product in sheet form.
Clean	Free from knots.
Clear	Free from visible defects and imperfections.
Density	Weight per unit volume such as lb per cubic ft or g per cubic cm.
Edge	Narrow side of square sawn timber.
End	Cross-cut surface of square sawn timber.
Face	Broad side of square sawn timber.
Figure	Ornamental markings, seen on cut surface of timber, formed by structural features of the wood.
Grain	General direction or arrangement of fibres. Plane of the cut surface, e.g. edge-grain, end-grain.
Lumber	Imported square edged sawn hardwood of random width. Also refers to all forms of sawn timber.
Machined	Having a surface or dimension that has been subject to machine operation after initial conversion.
Nominal	Size before planing. Planing will reduce the nominal thickness of a sawn board by about 3 mm ($\frac{1}{8}$in) and width by up to 6 mm ($\frac{1}{4}$in).
P1E	Planed one edge. P2E, planed two edges.
P1S	Planed one side. P2S, planed two sides.
P1S1E	Planed one side and one edge.
P4S	Planed four sides.

P.A.R.   Planed all round.
P.T.G.   Planed, tongued and grooved.
T. and G.   Re-sawn and machined boards to the general section
              shown in *Figure 1.5*. Much used for flooring.
Un-edged   Plank with both edges waney.

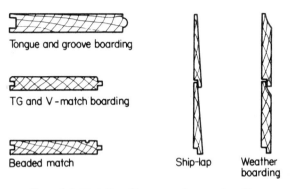

Tongue and groove boarding

TG and V-match boarding

Beaded match   Ship-lap   Weather
                                    boarding

Figure 1.5. Varieties of tongue and groove boarding

Man-made boards

Various composite boards are manufactured by quite involved
processes requiring complicated machinery, intricate production
lines and well organised factories. Probably the most common
is fibreboard, which includes the ubiquitous hardboard, so well
known it needs no description. Fibreboards range from fairly
thick low density boards (insulation board) through various
medium density boards to standard hardboard and finally
oil-tempered hardboard, which is so dense that it can be used
for external cladding and floor surfacing.

Fibreboard

This is made from wood and other ligneous materials after
they have been reduced to a fibrous pulp. This pulp is carefully graded, spread on 'mats' to a predetermined thickness,

pressed, dried and trimmed to standard size sheets. Various refinements in the general process described are added to produce the different qualities or grades.

Plywood

This is made from three or more thin laminations (or plies) of wood bonded together so that the grain of one ply is at right angles to its neighbour (*Figure 1.6*). Many grades are available according to type of wood used, whether surfaced

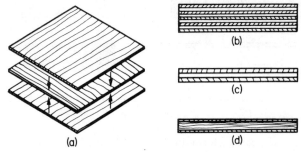

Figure 1.6. Plywood: (a) principle of construction, (b) multi-ply usually has an odd number of laminations, (c) 3-ply equal, which is stronger in one direction than the other, (d) 3-ply 'stout heart', which is of about equal strength in both directions

with a decorative veneer or not, thickness of laminations, quality of exterior surface, and type of glue used. Marine grade is made from best quality materials with water- and boil-proof glue.

Block-board, lamin-board and batten-board

These are composite boards with cores of solid softwood in the form of strips. The narrower the strips the less chance there is of distortion and surface undulations. It usually has birch faces and is frequently sold in veneered form.

Chipboard or particle board

In simple terms this is a board made from graded wood chips bonded together with an adhesive under great pressure and heat. Many manufacturers offer this material with veneered faces and edges in two or more standard lengths and up to ten widths from 152 mm (6 in) upwards. It is also available with melamine and other plastics surfaces. Chipboard, unveneered, is used for constructional work, including floors, and is manufactured to specific standards.

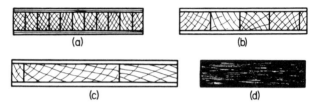

Figure 1.7. Composite boards: (a) lamin-board, (b) block-board, (c) batten-board, (d) veneer faced chipboard

Lamin-board, shown in *Figure 1.7 (a)*, is considered the best and most stable of the composite boards. The core strips, not more than 6mm ($\frac{1}{4}$ in) wide, are bonded together with the heart sides alternating. Lamin-board may have one or two outer plies. Block-board (*b*) has strips up to about 19 mm (¾ in) wide and also has one or two outer plies. Batten-board (*c*) has strips up to 76 mm (3 in) wide.

Veneer faced chipboard is shown in *Figure 1.7 (d)*. Often chips are graded from large ones in the centre to fine particles on the face. A point to watch is that in large particles screw-holding may be affected when edge fixing so it is advisable to use plugs specially made for chipboard.

Fixings and fittings

To assemble woodwork constructions, joints, glues, mechanical fixings and numerous fittings are needed. The most common fixing is the nail.

Wire nails are usually made from mild steel, but other metals are used for special purposes such as brass, gun metal or copper for boatbuilding. Diameter of the nail is referred to as the

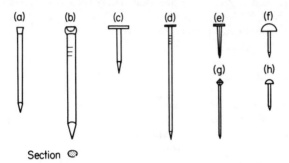

Figure 1.8. Nails: (a) panel pin, (b) oval, (c) clout, (d) wire or French nail, (e) tack, (f) upholstery nail, (g) hardboard nail, (h) escutcheon pin

gauge, and nails are sold by weight. The most common nails used today, illustrated in *Figure 1.8*, are now described.

Panel pins

These are used in light woodworking and cabinet making (*a*). Thin nails, with small heads that are easily punched below the surface, they are obtainable from 13 mm ($\frac{1}{2}$ in) to 51 mm (2 in) long.

Ovals

These are oval in section, with small heads easily punched below the surface (*b*). The oval section helps to prevent splitting of thin wood, especially near edges. They are made in many sizes and have many applications in general woodworking.

Clout

This is a round nail with a large head (*c*). Invariably galvanised to prevent rusting, they are used mainly for fixing roofing felt and similar fabrics to sheds and outbuildings, or underfelts and other membranes before tiling or slating roofs.

Round heads

These are sometimes known as wire nails or French nails (*d*). Heads are not usually punched in as they are designed to take much of the load and in many constructions the nail heads are not objectional. They can, however, be sunk with a stout punch or 'nail set' and the hole can be stopped prior to painting or other finish.

The chance of splitting wood being fixed is greatly reduced if the point is nipped off a wire nail or pin, or if the head is placed on an iron mass while the point is given a direct tap with a hammer. The nails then tend to punch a hole through the wood rather than force the fibres apart.

Tacks

Usually available from 13 mm ($\frac{1}{2}$ in) long and with a blued finish to prevent rusting (*e*), they have round heads for gripping fabrics such as upholstery materials or carpets. To make 'starting' easier, tacks have fine, needle-like points. A very thin type of tack, also used for upholstering, is called a gimp pin.

Upholstery nails

About 19 mm ($\frac{3}{4}$ in) long, they have a large, domed head, are usually made of steel and electro-brassed to provide a decorative effect and are used to fix finishing edges or strips in upholstery (*f*).

Hardboard pins

These are thin, square section copper or cadmium coated pins (*g*) with diamond shaped 'lost head', easily punched in for stopping.

Escutcheon pin

This is a small, domed head nail, usually brass, for pinning small metal plates to a surface (*h*).

Screws

Generally, screws provide a stronger fixing than do nails, but are more expensive and more preparation is required. Screws are the usual means of securing brassware, ironmongery and

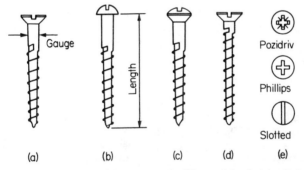

Figure 1.9. Screws: (a) countersunk, (b) round head, (c) raised head, (d) chipboard, (e) screwdriver patterns

other fittings. They are made in various metals, of which by far the most common is mild steel, followed by brass. They are also available in stainless steel and other hard, non-ferrous metals for marine and outside work, and aluminium alloy. Steel screws are sometimes finished with chrome and other deposited metals, or black enamel (japan).

They are made in many diameter sizes and lengths, and with different kinds of head (*Figure 1.9*). Gauge is the diameter of shank and length is measured from the widest diameter of the head to the tip of the point. Four common types of screw are: countersunk (csk) (*a*), round head (*b*), raised head (*c*) and csk chipboard screw (*d*). The extra thread on a chipboard screw provides more grip when fixing thin fittings.

Three screwdriver patterns are used (*Figure 1.9*) but the most common are slotted and Pozidriv. The Phillips is practically obsolete but a Pozidriv screwdriver can be used to drive Phillips pattern screws. A Phillips driver, however, should not be used for Pozidriv screws.

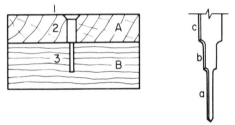

Figure 1.10. Preparation of wood for screwing (see text)

Where possible, screw fixing is done through the thinner material into the thicker (*Figure 1.10*). Preparation of two pieces of wood (A and B) for joining with a screw is shown: (1) is the countersink for csk screws, (2) is the clearance or shank hole and (3) is the pilot hole, which should be drilled first through both pieces if possible.

Special bits for drills, which bore the three sizes in one pass, are available for many screw sizes. The tip of such a drill is illustrated: (a) cuts the pilot hole, (b) cuts the shank hole and (c) the countersink.

Brass screws are soft and can easily shear off when being driven in, especially in a piece of close-grained hardwood. An old dodge is to initially insert a steel screw, then remove it and replace with a brass one. A scrape of candle wax or soap on the threads of large screws makes them go in much easier.

Pozidriv screws have a star-shaped recess in the head, instead of a slot. Main advantages are neatness, and far less chance of the screwdriver slipping and possibly damaging the surface. As with slotted screws, the correct size of screwdriver must be used in relation to the screw size.

Hinges

Many varieties of hinges are now available, including speciality hinges for step ladders and decorator's pasteboards, chipboard

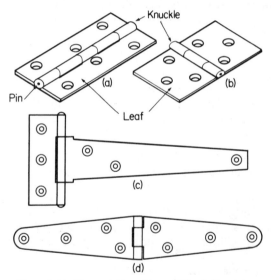

Figure 1.11. Hinges: (a) butt hinge, (b) back flap, (c) tee hinge (d) strap hinge

hinges, lay-on hinges and skeleton hinges which do not have to be housed in the hinged members. The more traditional types are still used every day (*Figure 1.11*). They include the following types.

Butt hinges, or butts   The best are of solid, cast brass and are used as door hinges on high quality cabinet and joinery work (*a*). Lighter patterns are available in pressed or folded brass. Cast iron butts are often used on heavy entrance doors and lighter, pressed steel butts are used for internal, domestic doors and other joinery. In all cases the pins are of steel or harder alloys. These hinges are usually sunk or 'housed' in the members, flush with the surface.

Back flaps   These are used where the wood is wide enough to take the leaves (*b*). This type of hinge, in brass or steel, enables the screws to be well spaced out, thus spreading the load and reducing chances of the wood splitting. They are also housed.

Tee hinges   These are usually in pressed steel, bright, or japanned (*c*). They are used mainly for exterior doors of ledged construction to sheds and outbuildings. Simple and strong, they are easy to fix and do not need to be housed in.

Strap hinges   This type can also be used for doors, but are much used on boxes and chests for storing tools, and so on (*d*).

Piano hinge   This is a thin, light hinge in the form of a continuous strip with leaves of about 13 mm ($\frac{1}{2}$ in) and screw holes every 50 mm (2 in) or so. This is also a surface fixed hinge used for boxes, light cupboard and wardrobe doors, in addition to piano lids.

Fittings

There are literally thousands of fittings made for woodworking, in addition to the usual knobs, bolts, catches and locks. Some fairly modern ones are shown in *Figure 1.12*.

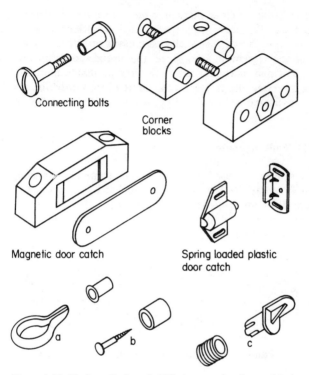

Connecting bolts

Corner blocks

Magnetic door catch

Spring loaded plastic door catch

Figure 1.12. Fittings. Various shelf fittings are also shown: (a) ring stem and sleeve, (b) stud, (c) insert and lug

Connecting bolts These are used to join two cabinets or box constructions, especially if they are likely to be dismantled at some future date.

Corner blocks These provide a simple means of making right-angled joints and are especially useful with chipboard constructions. Each half of the fitting is screwed to one of the pieces being joined. The two parts are then held together by a moulded-in nut and set screw.

Shelf fittings   Three popular types are shown. The ring stem
(*a*) fits in the sleeve, which is inserted in a drilled hole, two or
more to each side. The shelf is supported by the flat rings. The
stud (*b*) is simply screwed to the upright sides to provide
support and at (*c*) the insert fits in a pre-bored hole and the
lug is pressed into it. Inserts can be fitted in 'ladder' formation;
the inserts can then be varied to suit the shelf space required.

Woodworking terms

Many terms are used in woodworking; some have meanings in
our everyday life but others are peculiar to the craft and may
have different meanings in ordinary usage. Some of the more
common are listed; others will be introduced as they are used
in subsequent chapters.

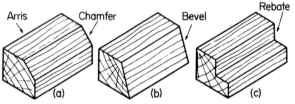

Figure 1.13. Terms applied to various edge treatments

Arris   A sharp edge of wood left when an angle is formed
(*Figure 1.13*). It is often rounded off or radiused to avoid
damage.

Chamfer   To remove an edge or corner for protection or
decoration. Normally the cut is made at 45 degrees, but this
angle can be varied. A chamfer is shown in *Figure 1.13(a)*.

Bevel   In some ways similar to a chamfer and often confused
with it, a bevel is where the whole edge is planed at an angle
other than 90 degrees (*b*).

Rebate Where the edge of a member is cut away in the form of a step it is said to be rebated. Surfaces of the rebate are normally parallel to the main surfaces (*c*), but can sometimes be bevelled.

Groove While a rebate is formed on the edge, the groove is formed away from the edge, as shown in *Figure 1.14(a)*, with the grain. Across the grain this cut is called a trench, or dado

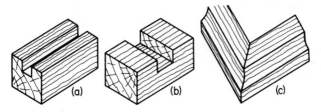

Figure 1.14. (a) Groove, (b) trench, (c) mitre

in American terms (*b*). When two corners are joined to conceal end grain the joint is called a mitre (*c*). This need not be at 90 degrees, as shown in the example.

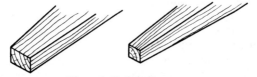

Figure 1.15. Simple tapers

Taper Simple tapers, as used on chair and table legs, are shown in *Figure 1.15*.

2 Tools

Good tools will last a lifetime and it is better to have a few tools of the right type and quality than a mass of third rate ones. Even in this age of machinery hand tools are indispensable and a woodworker's basic kit should include the following items.

Chisels

To start with, choose the bevelled edge firmer pattern (*Figure 2.1*) as this form enables the worker to get in to close corners and angles when trimming off, and paring off thin shavings when 'easing' a sinking, or cut. In the drawing (a) is the handle — these days made principally from high-density plastics material and formerly from boxwood or ash. The ferrule (b) prevents splitting of the handle and (c) is the tang which locates the chisel in its handle. The shoulder (d) prevents the tang from driving further into the handle. The bevel which gives the chisel its name is (e), while (f) is the grinding bevel and (g) is the honing or sharpening bevel. The tip of an ordinary firmer chisel is shown at (h) and (i) is that of the stouter mortise chisel.

Three sizes of chisel, 25, 13 and 6 mm (1, $\frac{1}{2}$, and $\frac{1}{4}$ in) are suggested as starters. New chisels should be sharpened before use; they are sold with only the grinding bevel applied. This is about 25 degrees, while the cutting bevel is about 30 degrees.

Chisels should be stored in a rack — blade guards, if available, should be used. This is to protect the easily damaged cutting edge. If a chisel has to be struck to do its cutting, hit it with a rubber, or wooden, mallet — never with metal hammers.

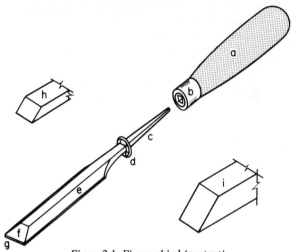

Figure 2.1. Firmer chisel (see text)

Mallet

Joiners' mallets are usually made of beech but other hard and dense woods may be used. Choose a medium size one for general use. Some workers make their own with square, rectangular or even round heads.

Marking gauge

A simple but much used tool for making lines with the grain and parallel to the face or edge of a workpiece *Figure 2.2*. The method of setting the gauge is shown in (*a*) and method of using is shown in (*b*). The stock of the gauge, which slides along the bar, is secured with a thumb screw, shown in (*a*).

Note that the gauge is tilted with the point just touching the work and held against the face edge. It is pushed away

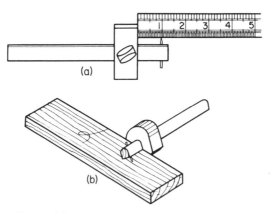

Figure 2.2. Marking gauge: (a) setting the gauge, (b) method of use

from the user and kept tight against the edge. The line should not be drawn over with a pencil. Always double check the setting before use.

Try-square

The traditional pattern, with a steel blade and wood or plastics stock, is shown in *Figure 2.3(a)* and the combination square, with a 305 mm (12 in) blade is illustrated at (*b*). This can be recommended as a tool with many uses without losing its efficiency as a try-square.

It can also be used for angles of 45 degrees and, because the blade is adjustable, it can be adapted for small or confined work which the fixed blade one will not. It can also be used as a marking gauge by holding a pencil against the blade and sliding both square and pencil along the work. Most combination squares have a small spirit level built into the stock.

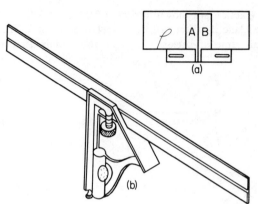

*Figure 2.3. Try-square: (a) testing for accuracy,
(b) combination square*

To test a try square for accuracy, scribe a line with the
square held as at A in *Figure 2.3(a)*, then reverse the square as
at B and scribe a line again. They should coincide, or be parallel.

Rules

It is advisable to have two types: a folding rule of rigid material
opening out to 1 m (39 in) is useful when working on the
bench while a flexible one of the steel tape type up to 3 m
(10 ft) is very handy when tackling bigger work or when
measuring up for a project around the home.

At the present time both imperial and metric units are in
use so it is just as well to buy rules with dual scales — metric
down one side and imperial down the other.

Tenon saw

This is the general purpose saw used for bench work, including
the cutting of most joints in woodwork. Tooth form and

cutting action are shown in *Figure 2.4(a)* and *(e)*. As the back of the blade is stiffened with a steel or brass 'back' (hence the general name of back-saw to such tools) it is used only for

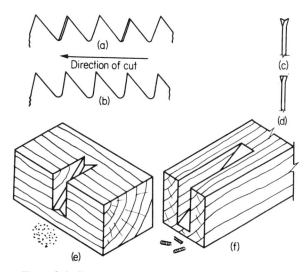

Direction of cut

Figure 2.4. Sawing: (a) tenon saw tooth form, (b) rip saw tooth form, (c) 'set' of tenon saw teeth, (d) 'set' of rip saw teeth, (e) tenon saw kerf, (f) rip saw kerf

straight cuts and care should be taken to prevent buckling of the blade. A popular size is one with a 254 mm (10 in) blade and 14 points per inch (PPI). Larger and smaller blade sizes are available.

Angles and shape of saw teeth affect their cutting. Tenon and most other saws have teeth shaped to the cross-cut pattern (*a*). Teeth are bent alternately right and left and the needle-like points scribe a double line across the wood on each stroke. The remaining edges push out the waste matter in the form of 'dust'. This bending is called the 'set' and is shown, exaggerated, at (*c*). In practice the setting is only sufficient to allow the blade to run without binding and varies according to the number of teeth there are to the inch. This tooth form will cut with the grain but for extensive with-the-grain cutting the rip saw and rip-form shaped teeth are used (*b*). Angles are also different, the teeth edges being flat and chisel-like as shown at (*d*) — not needle pointed. These chisel points produce small curly shavings and the cutting action with a sharp saw is quite rapid. The cut made by a saw is called the 'kerf'. The kerf made by a cross cutting saw is shown at (*e*) and that made by the rip saw is shown at (*f*).

All saws should be looked after with great care and blade guards should be used when they are not in use. It is also a good idea to hang them up, by the handle, on pegs or hooks.

When a saw becomes 'dull', points of the teeth look dull. When they become blunt, they should be re-sharpened. This is a fairly skilful operation and the beginner is advised to send his saws to a 'saw doctor' for professional attention. Good hardware stores usually provide this service.

Hammers

The two most popular types of hammer for woodworking are the Warrington pattern and the claw hammer. Although both are available in different sizes or weights of head the Warrington is generally used for lighter work and the claw for constructional work in heavy timbers. The claw is useful for withdrawing nails.

A 6 oz cross pein Warrington for general use and a 3½ oz one for light work — often called a pin-hammer — are to be recommended, and a 10 to 16 oz claw hammer for heavy work.

Planes

Metal planes have now almost completely replaced the wooden planes of former years. There are many different planes, quite a number for specialist use, and there is a range of bench planes — the two most frequently in use being the jack plane, about

356 mm (14 in) long and the smoothing plane, about 230 mm
(9 in). Different widths of blade are offered, the 51 mm (2 in)
being popular. For a beginner these two can be regarded as
interchangeable; apart from the obvious difference in length
the other differences are controllable by the user. One is the
shape of the cutting edge; some workers have two blades for
a jack plane, one for preparing sawn stuff and the other for
'smoothing'.

Part of a typical bench plane is illustrated in *Figure 2.5*. This
shows the front of the mouth, which prevents the wood from

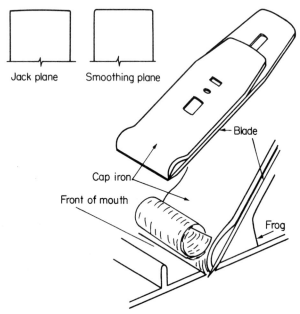

Figure 2.5. Bench plane

splitting ahead of the blade. The cap iron creases and coils the
shaving, and also stiffens the blade. This prevents the blade
from 'chattering' or vibrating. The cap iron is adjustable and
is set very close to the cutting edge for a smoothing plane and

rather less for a jack. The jack plane blade should be very slightly rounded or curved, while smoothing, block and similar planes have a straight edge. Corners of a smoothing plane are slightly rounded to prevent 'digging-in', caused by tilting the blade sideways when honing.

The mouth on a bench plane is adjustable for size; the smaller the mouth the less chance there is of tearing the grain, thus a better surface is made. A small mouth, however, will only allow the passage of fine,thin shavings. As the jack plane is often used for the quick removal of excess wood the shavings may be thicker; this is done by opening the mouth, a simple operation. After preparing work with the jack plane a smoothing plane may be used to bring up a fine finish. It is also used to clean up wide boards, which is why the edges are rounded slightly.

Sharpening planes and chisels

The sharp cutting edges of planes and chisels are imparted in the 'honing' process, carried out on an oil-stone (*Figure 2.6*), either natural or artificial. This is used with an oil; ideally, neatsfoot oil should be used but a light machine oil (lubricating) is frequently used. Never use an oxidising oil such as linseed. This would form a skin on the stone, clog up the pores and ruin it.

The main purpose of oil is to float away the minute particles of metal as the edge of the blade is worn away, so frequent oiling is needed. The stone may be completely cleaned from time to time with paraffin.

Many grades and shapes of stone are available. For general use a standard flat double-sided stone is best. One side is fine and the other coarse. The coarse side brings the edge up more quickly but it should be finished on the fine side.

For both planes and chisels the grinding angle (G) is about 25 degrees. To produce the cutting edge the angle is increased to about 30 degrees (H). When sharpening, always maintain as low an angle as possible, providing the tip of the edge is in contact with the stone. It is essential that the angle between blade and stone is consistent as even a slight backwards and forwards rocking action with the hands will produce a rounded bevel on the blade. Do not push the blade straight up and back

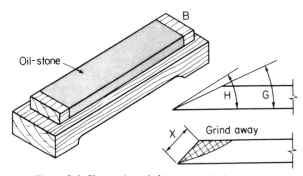

Figure 2.6. Sharpening of planes and chisels (see text)

but use a sideways, figure-of-eight motion which will help to induce even wear of the stone — a stone will wear out in time and a 'hollow' stone will need facing up, a difficult process.

Sharpening should continue until a slight burr is felt on the back of the blade. The blade is then carefully laid flat on its back and pushed across the stone to remove the burr. After many re-honings the grinding angle will be removed and the area being honed will be increased (X). Such a blade will need re-grinding.

Never form a bevel on the back of a chisel or plane blade as this will seriously affect the cutting action and will prevent the cap iron of a plane from seating properly. Stropping on a leather strop will remove any final trace of burr for really critical work but that careful back stroke across the oil stone should be sufficient. Ignore the so-called experts who advise stropping on the palm of the hand — it is a silly and dangerous practice.

An excellent general purpose stone which cuts fast and produces a keen edge is the India medium grit. Preferred size is 203 × 52 × 25 mm (8 × 2 × 1 in). The stone should be housed in a box and provided with a lid. Serious workers usually extend the stone at its ends with blocks of hard wood, fitted perfectly level with the stone surface (B). These blocks enable the stone to be used for the whole of its length, another aid to even wear.

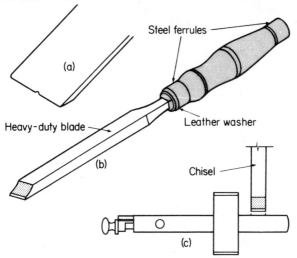

Figure 2.7. (a) Nicked blade, in need of grinding, (b) mortise chisel, (c) setting a mortise gauge

A number of honing guides are available and while they help a novice to keep to the bevel required it is better to practise 'free-hand' honing, maintaining an even pressure near the tip with fingers of one hand and holding the top of the blade or handle with the other. Watch that too much pressure is not applied to one side of the blade. This will cause an out-of-square end to the blade.

The purpose of grinding is simply to remove excess metal behind the honing bevel, otherwise honing will become a long, slow process. Blades which are 'nicked' as shown in *Figure 2.7(a)*, or otherwise damaged will also need grinding.

The most important point to guard against is the danger of overheating your steel when grinding on a modern high speed wheel. Overheating 'draws' the temper, causing the steel to go soft and lose its ability to hold a keen cutting edge. During grinding the blade should be frequently dipped in water; the whole operation should be carried out slowly, carefully and with gentle pressure. Sparks from a grinding wheel are really white to red hot fragments of metal — so do not make many.

For cutting mortises there are heavy duty chisels and if you intend to make many mortises it is just as well to obtain the ones you will need. A mortise chisel is shown in *Figure 2.7 (b)*. The blade is thicker than that of a firmer chisel and the handle is usually reinforced with a ferrule to take the constant mallet blows it will receive. There is also a shock absorber pad inserted over the shoulder. Note the grinding and honing bevels on the blade. When 'setting' a mortise gauge the pins are spaced to suit the chisel being used (*c*).

Additional tools

There is really no such thing as a complete kit of woodworking tools, so vast is the subject and so wide is the range of tools used to fashion the raw material into the many different projects that can be undertaken. However, the following are some of the tools most likely to be needed to augment the basic kit.

Brace

The two types of brace in use are the 'plain' and 'ratchet' (*Figure 2.8*). A useful size is one with a 254 mm (10 in) sweep. The ratchet mechanism enables drilling in spaces where a complete revolution of the handle is not possible. By adjusting the ratchet drive a forward or reverse movement of the bit is possible, or the drive can be locked to give drive in both directions, like a plain brace.

The jaws of a brace (*a*) will grip normal tapered square shanks of joiners' bits or the rounded shanks of morse pattern ones. Some popular types of bit are: Jennings pattern (*c*),

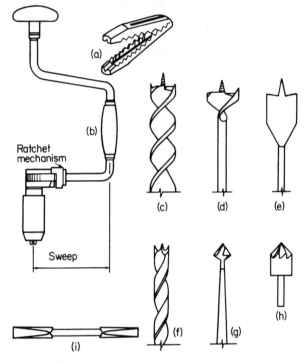

Figure 2.8. Brace and bits: (a) jaws of brace, (b) ratchet brace, (c) Jennings pattern bit, (d) screw-nosed centre bit, (e) flat bit for power drills, (f) lip and spur drill, (g) snail countersink, (h) wood or metal countersink, (i) double ended screwdriver bit

screw-nosed centre bit (*d*), flat bit for power drills (*e*), lip and spur drill (*f*), snail countersink (*g*), wood or metal countersink to fit all drills (*h*) and double ended screwdriver bit for the brace (*i*), which provides a powerful screwdriving force.

Wheelbrace

Although this is strictly an engineer's tool the wheelbrace is useful to a woodworker for boring small holes with standard twist and morse pattern drills. It can also be used for various metalworking jobs associated with woodworking. A chuck size of 8 mm ($^5/_{16}$ in) is to be preferred.

Brace bits

Many different types and patterns are available but the Jennings pattern is a good, all-round boring tool. It cuts a clean, deep hole and does not wander when knots or wild grain is encountered. The spurs, screws and cutting edges of bits must be protected, and kept sharp with a fine file. Wrapping them in baize-lined canvas is a good and simple way of looking after the bits; tool rolls made from canvas and baize can be bought if your stock builds up but bits should be purchased as the need arises − it is possible to buy a large set and never use half of them.

For large holes or occasional use the screw-nosed centre bit is a cheaper alternative to a Jennings but the bit should be withdrawn frequently to clear the hole being bored.

Other types of bit include the expansive, which can be adjusted within a good size range to bore various diameters in soft wood, and the Forstner, used for shallow and over-lapping holes, and for 'blind' holes where a lead screw would penetrate the surface.

Two types of bit have been specially developed over recent years for use in power drills. They are the flat bit (for larger holes) and the lip-and-spur bit, which is particularly suitable for making the smaller holes used for dowel joints. They fit in the various dowel jigs available without wobbling or wandering. It is, however, essential that metric drills are used in metric jigs, and imperial in imperial ones.

Screwdrivers

At least two cross-point screwdrivers and perhaps two Pozidriv ones will be needed. Drivers must be selected to fit the screw size. There is a large range of cross points but only four Pozidriv. Although the drivers are sized according to the length

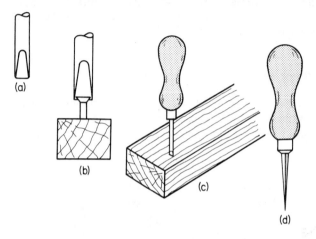

Figure 2.9. (a) Screwdriver blade with filed corners, (b) a blade which is too wide for the size of screw, (c) use of a bradawl, (d) birdcage pattern bradawl

of blade the critical dimension is the width and thickness of the cross-point tip. If too wide, as in *Figure 2.9 (b)*, it can cause damage to the work being screwed, and if too narrow it will not be possible to impart the 'drive' needed. Also, if the fit is 'sloppy' the driver can slip out of the slot, with unfortunate results. It is a good idea to file off the corners of a cross-point driver (*a*) and use a file to dress the tip so that it is a good fit in the screw slot.

With Pozidriv such problems do not arise; sizes 2 and 3 will drive a good range of screws but they should have pilot holes to assist entry.

Bradawls

Rather like a small screwdriver, the bradawl is used to bore
pilot holes for smaller screws. To use one, the blade is placed
across the grain, then the tool is twisted in the hand and pushed
into the wood (*c*). They are easily sharpened with a smooth
file. The birdcage pattern, with square, tapered and pointed
blade, is preferred by some workers and is especially handy
when using small screws (*d*).

Cutting gauge

The cutting gauge illustrated in *Figure 2.10* is used mainly for
marking across the grain, while the marking gauge (*Figure 2.2*)
is used with the grain, and the mortise gauge is used to mark

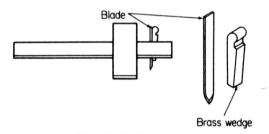

Blade

Brass wedge

Figure 2.10. Cutting gauge

double lines with the grain. Because of its blade profile the
cutting gauge can also be used for 'slitting' or cutting strips of
veneer and thin plywood.

Dovetail saw

For fine work the dovetail saw is ideal. This is a smaller version
of the back saw, but only about 203 mm (8 in) in length and
with smaller teeth and thinner blade.

Panel saw

This is used for cutting sheet material such as hardboard, plywood and composite boards, or wood which is not too thick.
Although the teeth are sharpened and formed primarily for
cross-cut use the saw will function reasonably well in any grain
direction. Popular size is 560 mm (22 in) long with 9 points
to the inch.

Saws for curves

The most useful saw in this group is the coping saw, shown in
Figure 2.11 (a), which cuts quite well in wood up to about
19 mm ($^3/_4$ in) thick. The blade is held taut with the spring-
steel frame. Lever bars, which can be turned to adjust the

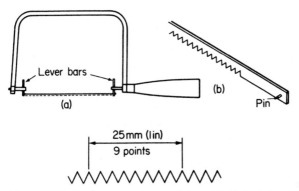

*Figure 2.11. Coping saw: (a) general view, (b) blade design,
(c) tooth size*

blade in the frame, must always be aligned the same way to
avoid blade distortion and bad cutting. A section of the blade
is shown at (*b*), illustrating the directional slope of the teeth
and anchor pin, which fits in a slot in the lever bar. Tension
of the saw is given by the handle, which is threaded to the
lever bar arm.

Experts argue as to whether the teeth should point away from the handle, thus giving the cut on the forward stroke, or towards the handle, when the cut will be on the backward stroke. In practice users find which method is applicable to a particular job. This saw is well suited to cutting out the waste on common dovetail joints.

Spokeshaves

These are really a kind of planing tool and remove shavings in a similar manner to a plane. They are used to smooth or round

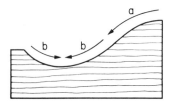

Figure 2.12. Use of spokeshave
(see text)

off the edges of curved work. There are many types but are divided into flat-faced and round-faced patterns. As shown in *Figure 2.12*, flat faces are used for straight work and external curves (a) while the round face is used for internal curves (b).

3 Basic Processes

Even though wood is often bought ready planed, or machined, in one form or another it is frequently necessary to prepare the timber to non-standard sizes in the workshop. If the timber is received 'sawn' then it must be prepared before it can be used.

Preparation includes reducing all the wood needed to required sizes by sawing and planing. For as long as can be established the planing and preparation of wood by hand has followed the same basic principles, with the same basic terminology and guide marks.

First the 'face side' is established. The better side of the timber is selected. It is then planed smooth and flat, tested with a straight-edge lengthways, crossways and cornerways until it is right. A face mark is then pencilled on it with the tail starting from the face edge, as in *Figure 3.1 (a)*.

The 'face edge' is next prepared, planed and tested with straight-edge and try-square, held tight against the face side; finally it is marked with the face edge mark (*b*).

Your timber is now gauged and planed to the required width. Gauge from the face edge, across the face side and underside to the required width, holding the gauge stock firmly to the face edge. Plane off the waste, testing frequently as before (*c*).

Now the timber is gauged to the required thickness on both edges, and ends, holding the gauge on the face side. Waste is then planed off, testing as before (*d*).

Usually the next step after planing is to mark out the length, although whether or not the waste at the ends is removed at this stage depends on the nature of the job.

When planing along the grain always plane with it, not against, otherwise tearing and digging-in may occur. The run of the grain is easy to see on the edge of the section. If the wood is planed on the end grain in a similar manner to

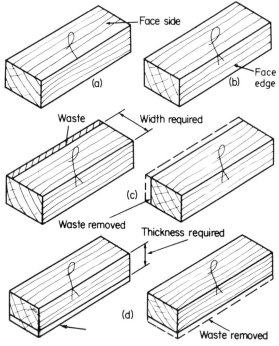

Figure 3.1. Preparation: (a) marking the face side, (b) marking the face edge, (c) gauging and planing to the required width, (d) gauging and planing to the required thickness

how it is planed on the edges then it is almost certain to split at the far edge. This is because the wood cannot adequately resist the pressure of the blade, and the splitting takes place where the wood is weakest — near the edge, as shown in *Figure 3.2 (a)*. If the wood can be supported at the corner, so that the edge cannot be forced outwards, then splitting will not occur.

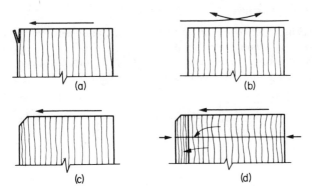

*Figure 3.2. Planing on end grain: (a) splitting, (b) prevention
by careful use of plane, (c) prevention by corner removal,
(d) prevention by addition of scrap piece*

When wood is planed on end grain it is usually referred to
as 'shooting'. The following methods are ways of doing this
which will prevent splitting.

1. Planing in both directions but not allowing the plane to
complete the stroke and reach the far corner (*b*).

2. Removing the corner. This can only be done if the
removal of the corner is of no consequence, perhaps because
of subsequent shaping (*c*).

3. Cramping scrap wood on workpiece. The scrap wood, in
effect, extends the width of the wood and any splitting will
therefore be in the scrap piece. If the scrap is chamfered
then even this is not likely to split (*d*).

4. Using a shooting board. This is a very satisfactory method
providing the wood is not too large. If the shooting board is
accurate the wood is not only planed, but it is finished
square and true.

As end grain offers greater resistance to the plane it is
essential for all end grain cutting that the plane is kept very
sharp.

Cutting a trench

Making a trench is a fairly simple operation and forms the basis of a number of joints: housing, bridle and half-laps of various kinds. When using a saw to cut joints the cut (kerf) must be on the waste side of the line (*Figure 3.3*).

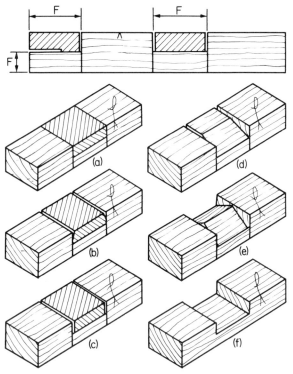

Figure 3.3. Cutting a trench: (a) marking off, (b) chiselling of V-grooves, (c) sawing, (d) and (e) chiselling away waste, (f) levelling off

Dimensions (F) represent the finished size of parts of the joints being made. (Joints are used in woodworking to provide greater mechanical strength, help hold the assembly together, provide greater gluing areas, give smooth flowing lines in design detail and to conceal end grain.)

The width of the trench is made exactly equal to the width or thickness of the part fitting into it, and is best if initially squared in with a pencil. That part of the joint which is actually going to be cut can be gone over with a marking knife. A marking knife lightly cuts the surface and gives a more accurate mark to work from, and working this way also gives an opportunity to check the precise width needed. A gauge is used to mark the depth. Remember to have the stock against the face side when gauging. The sequence of procedure is shown in *Figure 3.3.*

First mark off the trench, squared across, in pencil (*a*). Mark the depth of the trench with a gauge. Go over the lines, where actual cutting is to take place, with a marking knife then chisel in small V-grooves on waste side of lines (*b*). Saw down to the gauge mark, using V-grooves as guides for the saw, which must cut on the waste side of the line (*c*).

Chisel away waste at one side. Use as large a chisel as possible. Keep the flat side of the chisel down to the work and cut by pointing upwards on one side (*d*). Repeat this stage, working from the opposite edge (*e*). Level off the remainder of the waste by working inwards from the edges (*f*).

This is the type of trench used for half-lap joints and is half the thickness of the member. Trenches for other purposes are usually made one third of the thickness.

A stopped trench (*Figure 3.4*) is often used for bookcase shelves and similar work. It is marked out as described for a through trench, using a gauge to mark the limit of the 'stop' (*a*). Marking knife and chisel are used to make V-grooves (*b*), then a mortise is cut with the chisel at the 'blind' end of the trench (*c*). This allows sawing along the V-grooves to be carried out (*d*). Waste is then chiselled away with the back of the chisel down and initial cuts made as in *Figure 3.3 (d)* gradually decreasing the angle of chisel until a good start is made along the trench. Ideally a router should be used to level off the bottom of the trench but this tool has not yet been described and careful use of a sharp bevel-edge chisel should produce a satisfactory 'bottom'. The completed trench is shown at (*e*).

Perhaps the most traditional joint of all, employed by stonemasons and blacksmiths as well as woodworkers, is the

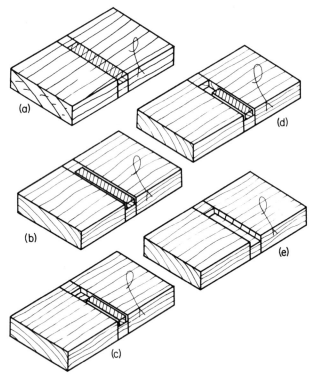

Figure 3.4. Stopped trench: (a) marking off, (b) chiselling of V-grooves, (c) forming a mortise, (d) sawing along V-grooves, (e) completed stopped trench

mortise and tenon. It is probably more widely used than any other joint in woodwork, and has variations of one sort or another that are almost countless. Its basic forms, though, are quite simple (*Figure 3.5*).

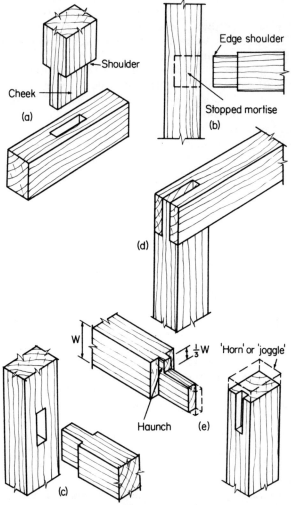

Figure 3.5. Mortise and tenon joints: (a) simple form, (b) stopped, (c) joint for wood of unequal size, (d) open mortise or corner bridle, (e) haunched

For very simple work tenon edge shoulders are not usually included. For furniture projects, edge shoulders are often incorporated as they completely seal, and conceal, ends of the mortise. With wide pieces the tenon is normally made in the form of a double tenon.

The shoulder of a tenon is marked with a marking knife and the location of the mortise is made in pencil. Thickness of the actual joint is gauged with a mortise gauge. Corresponding parts of the same joint should be marked at the same time, while the gauge is 'set'.

Ideally, a mortise gauge should have the distance between the pins set directly from the chisel which will be used for cutting the mortise. This is because chisels vary slightly in size and their widths are frequently not exactly what they are specified to be.

In its most simple form the mortise is cut right through the wood and the tenon has side shoulders but not edge shoulders, as in *Figure 3.5 (a)*. A blind or stopped mortise and tenon is shown at (b). Small, usually about 3 mm ($\frac{1}{8}$ in), shoulders are also introduced to conceal ends of the mortise.

Where the wood being joined is of unequal size, thickness of tenon can be increased above the usual one third rule, as in (c).

An open mortise, also known as a corner bridle, is shown in (d). This is a simple joint often used in framing.

More involved, and stronger, the haunched mortise and tenon is also used in frame construction. In practice it is usual to allow a little extra on the length of the mortised member to add strength during handling. This 'horn' or 'joggle' is cut off after assembly or when the frame is positioned (e).

Double tenons are made when the part to be tenoned is considerably wider than the part to be mortised, as in *Figure 3.6*. A long mortise, in relation to the thickness of the part, would weaken the joint (a). In addition to gluing, the joint can be further secured by wedges (b) which should have a slope of about 1 : 7. Ends of mortises are cut on a complementary slope to provide 'wedge' room (W). Screws or dowels can also be inserted (X).

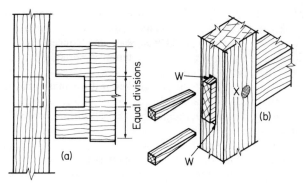

Figure 3.6. (a) Double tenon, (b) addition of wedges and dowel

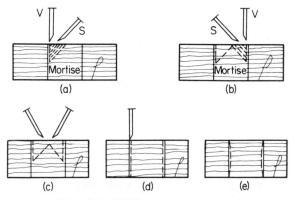

Figure 3.7. Chiselling a mortise (see text)

Mortises can be formed either entirely by chisel or the bulk of the waste can be removed by a chisel after the centre has been bored out with brace and bit. The bit must be smaller in diameter than the width of the mortise and the holes must not touch the sides of the mortise.

The procedure when chiselling out a mortise is shown in *Figure 3.7*. A series of vertical (V) and sloping (S) cuts are made, just inside the lines, about halfway through the wood (a) and (b). Extra sloping cuts are made in the centre part to level off the bottom (c). The work is then reversed and the first three steps are repeated. The chisel is now placed exactly on the line; the remaining waste is trimmed away, as in (d). Check that the ends of the mortise are not rounded (e) as this would give a false sense of tightness, when in fact the tightness is located at the centre. Remember that all surfaces in contact should have parallel sides.

Tenons are normally cut by sawing, with the saw just touching the line on the waste side. It is better to make the cuts with the grain first, followed by sawing the shoulders as, otherwise, some of the marking out may be lost if the side of the tenon is completely removed before all the cuts down the grain have been made. It is better to rasp away any excess rather than cut it away with a chisel.

When sawing a tenon, work is held upright in the vice. The saw is started in a corner on the waste side of the line, as shown in *Figure 3.8 (a)*. The handle of the saw is lowered as sawing continues (b) without the front of the saw cutting any deeper (far line cannot be seen during sawing). Now slope the wood slightly in the vice and continue sawing by lowering the handle until the shoulder line is reached (c). Reverse the wood in the vice, but keep it vertical, and continue sawing, keeping the saw level, until the shoulder line is reached (d). The sequence of cutting on a tenon with edge shoulders is shown in (e).

The bridle joint is in many ways similar to the mortise and tenon, but with the 'opposite' parts cut away, as shown in *Figure 3.9 (a)*. It is the joint usually adopted where a piece has to be jointed to a component which is thinner. Care should be taken to see that the joint is not made too tight, or the forked parts will tend to be forced outwards, which can even result in splitting.

The dovetail joint, when correctly made, is a very strong joint as, by the nature of the slope it resists attempts to pull it apart except in the way it was assembled. A dovetail halving joint is illustrated in *Figure 3.9 (b)*. This is the most simple

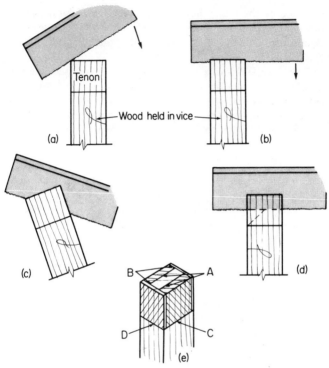

Figure 3.8. Sawing a tenon (see text)

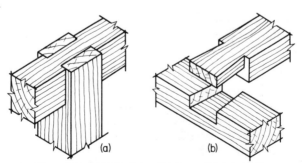

Figure 3.9. (a) Bridle joint, (b) dovetail halving joint

variation of the joint, the basis of which is the sloping part of the joint which resembles the tail of a dove. Because of the slope this joint can only be assembled in one direction and will resist being pulled apart in any other.

The dovetail halving and variations of it are used in frame, or 'flat', construction while the common, or box dovetail — as its name suggests — is used for box or 'carcase' constructions.

Dovetailing is easiest if carried out from a squared off end, as the extent or limit of the joint can then be readily marked

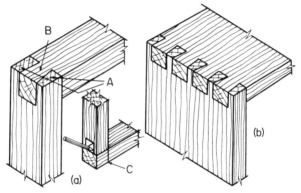

Figure 3.10. (a) Single dovetail joint, (b) common or box dovetail joint

with a cutting gauge. There are more ways of cutting the joint than one but most craftsmen cut the pins first, following the method shown in *Figure 3.10*. By standing the piece with the pins on the opposite member and marking around them with a well pointed pencil the exact size, shape, slope and position of the corresponding tails or 'sockets' can be accurately marked out. This means that for something like a simple box or frame the marking out must be done so that all four pieces will properly fit together. Face side and edge marks on all work and individual labelling of each half of each joint, will help to prevent errors.

The single dovetail joint, shown in *Figure 3.10 (a),* is much used in framing. Pins are indicated (A) and (B) is the tail. It is usual to cut the pins first. The tail is then marked directly from the pins, as shown, after having squared or gauged in the guide line (C). Corresponding parts of dovetail joints are usually individually 'tailored' in this fashion.

Common or box dovetails follow the same basic pattern (*b*) as do the single dovetails. It is more satisfactory and gives a better joint if a pin is arranged to come at the edge, and not a tail.

The work sequence when forming dovetail pins is shown in *Figure 3.11 (a).* First shade in the waste to avoid errors in sawing (A). Next, saw down the grain on the waste side of the line (B). Cut out the bulk of the waste with a coping saw (C),

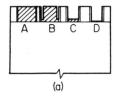
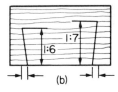

Figure 3.11. (a) Work sequence for forming dovetails, (b) dovetail angles

keeping just clear of the line going across the grain. This line is usually made with a cutting gauge. Chisel away the remainder of the waste, checking that surfaces are flat and square (D).

The angle at which a dovetail is cut must be considered: if it is too slight the joint will tend to slide out, and if it is too great there is a danger that the corners of the tail will break away. By long usage and practice it has been established that the angle should be about one in seven. That is, if the tail is seven units long it should be one unit wider at the end than at the base, as shown in *Figure 3.11 (b).* If the wood is hard and close grained a slightly smaller angle can be employed, but the limit at all times is considered to be one in eight.

4 Workshop Practice

A methodical, disciplined approach to work is essential if accuracy and fine workmanship are to be achieved. Whatever the job may be it has to be 'set out', parts have to be prepared and identified, cut to size and test assembled.

Setting out

In many cases the project will be in the form of a prepared plan, with or without a descriptive article, and a parts or cutting list. Do not rush blindly into cutting parts from a list before first checking carefully. Look over the drawings. Check measurements on them, then check the list. If it is possible, make a full size drawing from the scale details, then check for cutting. Timber is costly these days and an error in cutting can waste a lot of valuable material. There is still an old saying, doubly true these days: 'Measure twice, cut once'.

To give an example of setting out and preparing a job let us consider a typical small project for the home or school workshop. *Figure 4.1* shows the stages of setting out for a small corded-seat stool which has the same elevation on all four sides (*a*). The stool is 305 × 305 × 305 mm (12 in square). Legs are 32 mm (1¼ in square). Top rails are 32 × 19 mm (1¼ × ¾ in) and the bottom rail is 25 × 19 mm (1 × ¾ in) placed 76 mm (3 in) from lower ends of legs.

The basic procedure, which generally is the same on all projects, is first to place all legs together in the vice, with ends approximately level and face sides and edges arranged as shown in (*b*). Then carry out all gauging, squaring, marking and measuring from these surfaces.

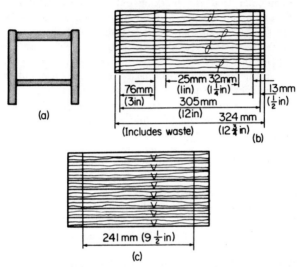

Figure 4.1. Setting out for a small stool: (a) elevation of stool, (b) marking out the legs, (c) marking out the rails

Next, mark out all similar pieces, together, while they are held in the vice or cramps. This is not only quicker but far more accurate than marking each piece separately.

Do not forget that there are often right hand and left hand parts to a job, therefore, when doing the marking out arrange the face marked components in pairs. *Figure 4.1 (b)* shows the legs of the stool arranged in pairs although, in this case, they are all the same. Marking out for the rails is shown in (*c*).

Reference has frequently been made to a marking knife. There is a tool by this name, with a pointed and bevel-edge blade. But a trimming knife of the Stanley type can be used to mark out, and this has other uses. Where sawing has to be done across the grain use a marking knife, or a sharp pencil of moderate hardness, say 2H. Mark out all corresponding pieces for that part of the job at the same time, before doing any sawing.

Remember that the marking out for one part of a joint must correspond exactly with the other part, and not be made slightly bigger or smaller. Always shade in the waste. It is so easy to cut out the wrong part of a joint, or even saw on the wrong side of a line.

Returning to the rails (c), place them in the vice, ends level and face edges up. Square across to the dimension given. This dimension is known as the shoulder length. In this case it is arrived at by subtracting the thickness of two legs from the length: $305 - (2 \times 32) = 241$ mm, or $12 - (2 \times 1\frac{1}{4}) = 9\frac{1}{2}$ in.

Check and re-check all marking out. An accurately cut joint will not fit if it is made in the wrong part of the wood. Acknowledge that old saying 'measure twice, cut once' without having to learn it the hard way!

Slight alternatives are possible in the positions of the rails, and therefore the joints, as shown in *Figure 4.2 (a)*. One is central, the other is offset. The latter gives slightly longer tenons.

With a mortise gauge mark in the tenon size (b), and gauge from the face side, setting the gauge to the chisel you will use. For gauging the legs, pins of the gauge are not changed but the stock must be moved to give either a central mortise or an offset one, as shown in (c).

The kinds of errors that can occur when setting out are shown in (d). Incorrectly squared lines around the work (A) is one. Lines should meet at every corner. At (B) the gauge lines do not align on edge of end, probably because the gauge was not set with pins central, or the gauge was not always kept tight against the face side.

In (e) the gauge lines are correct on the face side but not on the face edge. Correct position is shown dotted. This error arises through failure to keep the gauge stock against either the face side or the face edge.

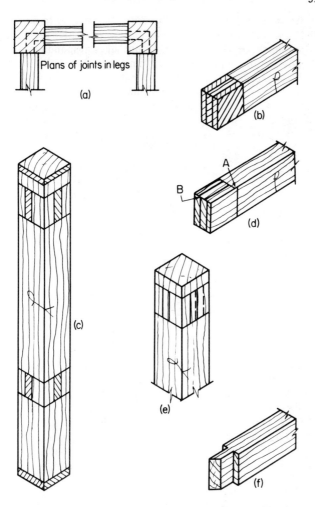

Figure 4.2. Forming the joints for a small stool: (a) plan showing alternatives for rail positions, (b) marking out the tenon, (c) marking out the legs, (d) errors which can occur when setting out, (e) gauge lines are correct on face side but not on face edge, (f) completed tenon with edge mitred

After tenons have been sawn they must be cut to length and also have their ends mitred (*f*). Both can be done on a mitre block or in a mitre box. Length of tenons must be slightly less than depth of mortise.

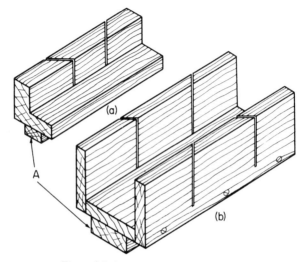

Figure 4.3. (a) Mitre block, (b) mitre box

The mitre block, shown in *Figure 4.3 (a)* can be used for mitring small section material where accuracy is not too critical. A mitre box (*b*) is used for larger size work and provides better control of the saw (which should fit closely in the slots) and is therefore more accurate. Either can be purchased or made in the workshop (see Chapter 5 for construction details). Blocks screwed to the base (A) provide a grip for the vice.

Cleaning up

Assembling the parts, cleaning up, securing the assembly and applying the finishes are stages that logically follow setting out. No matter how well made a joint may be, a light stroke with a plane, rub with glasspaper or some other cosmetic operation is needed to enhance the appearance of the work before applying polish, varnish or whatever the final process may be.

Cleaning up is the process of removing all pencil and other marks from the work, making the surfaces smooth, and

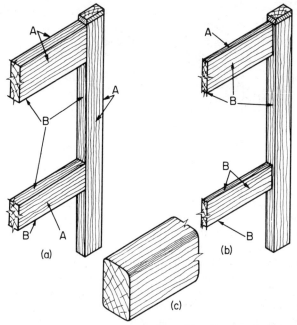

Figure 4.4. Cleaning up procedure: (a) rails same thickness as legs, (b) rails thinner than legs, (c) arris removed

preparing the job for the application of the 'finish'. Broadly, cleaning up is carried out with a smoothing plane, followed by glasspapering, as in *Figure 4.4*.

Joggles or horns are usually left on until after assembly, then removed (*a*) and (*b*). In (*b*) the rails are thinner than the legs so the cleaning up procedure is slightly different.

Rails are cleaned up on their faces before assembly and joints do not have to be levelled as in (*a*). Outer surfaces of legs can be cleaned up before or after assembly.

Removing the arris with plane or glasspaper gives the professional touch, is more pleasant to the hands and lessens the chance of bruising or damage to a corner (*c*), but when

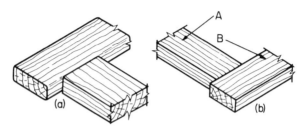

Figure 4.5. (a) Error to avoid when removing arris at a joint, (b) glasspapering around a joint

removing arrises care is needed to avoid the situation shown in *Figure 4.5 (a)* where the arris has been removed at a joint, resulting in an unsightly gap.

When glasspapering around a joint part (A) should be done first, always finishing with part (B). This helps to reduce the amount of cross-grain papering, and therefore scratching.

To do its job effectively the smoothing plane should be kept quite sharp, with the blade, cap iron and mouth prepared as described earlier. The aim with the smoothing plane is to skim over the work so that everywhere is covered, and yet the minimum of wood is actually removed. A close eye should be kept on the surface as planing proceeds to see if there is any tearing of grain. Any tendency of the fibres to tear can usually be corrected by reversing the work and thereby, in effect, planing the opposite way.

Glasspaper varies in its granule size, from 'flour' (00 grade), which is very fine, to 'strong 2' (S2), which is coarse. For most work two grades are sufficient, starting with either grade M2 or F2 and completing with grade $1\frac{1}{2}$ or 1. The following points should be noted when glasspapering.

1. Use a cork, rubber or wood block to support the paper. Do not work over flat surfaces with the paper held in the hand.

2. Hold the work firmly, either in a vice or cramped to the bench top.

3. Apply plenty of pressure; working slowly this way is much more effective, and far less tiring, than trying to do the job hurriedly.

4. Work with the grain whenever possible. Working across the grain, especially with coarse glasspaper, will scratch the surface and this will show up under a clear finish. Direction of working is not so important for a painted finish.

5. Do not glasspaper joints. A poor fitting joint is not improved by glasspaper and a good joint can easily be spoiled.

Other types of abrasive paper are available but they all do the same job and are used in the same manner as glasspaper. An exception is 'wet-and-dry' paper, which should not be used directly on a raw wood surface.

By the very nature of its purpose the cleaning up stage comes towards the end of a job when all the joints, shaping, cutting and fitting have been carried out. However, it cannot always be left until last and, broadly,the following is the procedure:

Before assembly, clean up those parts which cannot be reached after they have been put together. Those parts which can be tackled by plane and glasspaper after assembly are left until the work is glued up. This stage will often include levelling off joints and adjusting surfaces.

Assembling

Occasionally work is assembled without adhesives but for the vast majority of jobs glue of one sort or another is employed.

Scotch, or bone, glue is rarely used these days as it has many disadvantages compared with modern glues; it is still used by some craftsmen for special jobs such as veneering.

PVA (polyvinyl acetate) adhesive, which is a white emulsion that dries to a clear transparent film, is a good general-purpose woodworking assembly glue and is widely used. It is bought ready for use and is applied cold. This adhesive provides a satisfactory bond with materials allied to woodworking such as cork, leather and fabrics, and is clean and simple to use. It is not a waterproof glue however and is therefore limited to indoor use. It will also cope with plastics laminates, but only if pressure is applied over all the surface until the glue sets.

A more satisfactory adhesive for bonding plastics laminates to wood is one of the many 'impact' or 'contact' types. Makers' instructions must be followed and the result should be a bond so successful that it is impossible to break. Impact adhesive can also be used for veneering but it is not the best glue for normal assembly work.

For external work, and boatbuilding in particular, special resin-type glues are used. They are completely waterproof and are usually bought in powder form. They may be 'one-part' which incorporates a hardener, or 'two-part' where the hardener is separate.

Epoxy resins, usually sold in two-tube packs of resin and hardener, are useful for special applications of bonding metal surfaces to wood, or other dissimilar materials.

For most jobs, and especially for the man with little experience, it is advisable to have a trial run of assembling a piece of work with everything fitted 'dry'. This means that the work can be checked to ensure that it will, in fact, go together correctly, and with joints that are not too tight. While so assembled, it is advisable to mark each part of each joint so that when gluing the work will be re-assembled the same way.

For use when assembling, a simple form of squaring lath is shown in *Figure 4.6 (a)*. This is simply a strip of wood with one end pointed. The point fits in one internal angle and the diagonally opposite angle is marked on the other end of the lath. The lath is then reversed to the other angles and if the frame is square the mark will coincide. A better pattern is shown at (*b*) where two pointed laths slide over each other. They can then be held together and transferred to the other angles.

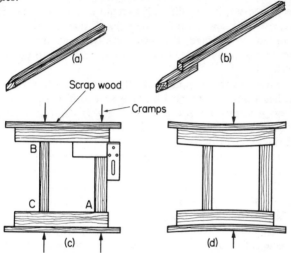

Figure 4.6. Squaring: (a) simple squaring lath, (b) a better pattern of squaring lath, (c) cramping and checking with a try-square, (d) bowing caused by incorrect cramping

Small frames can be checked with a try-square (*c*). Check also corners A, B and C. Cramps should be applied as indicated by arrows and scrap wood should be used under the cramps to protect faces of the work.

Bowing of sides can occur as the result of using a single cramp in the centre of the job (*d*), or when cramps are incorrectly positioned. Thick pads of wood also reduce the chances of bowing.

Being methodical is one of the essential disciplines of assembly work. Such cramps as are to be used should be set out and prepared at the 'dry-run' stage and scrap wood pads collected to place between jaws and work to prevent bruising and marking. Nails, screws, wedges or pegs to be used during assembly should be set out on the bench beforehand. In addition a container of clean water and some cloth swabs should be to hand for wiping off surplus glue before it hardens. Glue, once set, is very difficult to remove and if any smears of glue, however slight, dry out on parts that are to be clear varnished or polished, they will 'grin' through the polish as areas of a different shade to the natural wood colour you hope to achieve.

PVA glue can be applied directly from its plastics container if it has a nozzle, or with a brush or spatula if in a can. Do not be too generous but also do not be 'greedy'. Apply enough to wet all contacting areas without a lot of excess which will have to be mopped off later.

After applying the glue, check and cramp up without delay. Makers specify an 'open' time for their adhesives and usually it is slow enough to allow plenty of time for correct assembly. But the sooner the work is assembled and at rest for setting the better will be the bond. If things do go wrong, dismantle, mop off the glue while it is still wet, and start again. Partially set glue will not give a good bond. By the same token an incorrectly glued up assembly can rarely be put right once the glue has set.

Do not forget that cramps can exert a great deal of pressure. Use just enough to hold the assembly firmly — too much can distort the work.

As shown in *Figure 4.7 (a)* a frame which is out of square can be corrected by the slight re-positioning of one or both cramps, as indicated by the arrows. When the right-hand cramp is tightened it will pull the corner over, thus correcting the misalignment.

In (b) a frame which is badly twisted, or 'winding', is shown. Here, ends of cramps must be moved vertically up or down in order to pull the frame free from twist.

To test for correct alignment sight with the eye, as in (c). Surfaces of rails are in line. When viewed at right angles to the first observation point the legs should also be in alignment. The whole frame should be flat, or 'out of winding'.

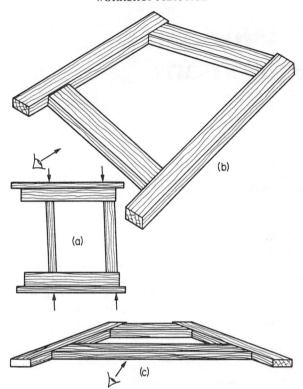

Figure 4.7. (a) Correction of out of square frame by re-positioning of cramps, (b) a badly twisted frame, (c) testing for correct alignment

All this is the counsel of perfection. It may sound formidable but in reality it is not; just the application of some common sense, patience and pride in achievement.

5 Workshop Equipment

Basic workshop requirements

A lot of woodworking projects can be done in a spare room, shed, garage, or even kitchen; for such activities there are many ingenious folding benches, including the Black and Decker Workmate bench. But, for more serious work and certainly if long periods of activity are expected a proper workshop is a necessity. It should have a good, level and dry floor, with walls strong enough to support shelves, racks and storage cupboards.

Figure 5.1 provides some idea of the minimum set-up needed for non-professional use but much depends on what the main interests will be. If large units of built-in furniture are going to be made then an area for pre-assembly is desirable. An outward opening door (A) creates less restriction on floor space than an inward opening door (B). An outward opening pair of doors (C) is advantageous where biggish work is tackled. It is also helpful if the door(s) are positioned so as to open opposite the line of the vice (D). Thus when long timber is worked in the vice it can project through the open door. Small woodworking machines may be acquired later, such as the universal woodworker, circular saw bench, lathe or bandsaw. Floor space will be needed for them. A simple rack, for holding saws, G-cramps etc., is also shown.

Many amateurs work quite comfortably in a shop or shed about 3 m × 2.5 m (10 ft × 8 ft) floor area or even less, but

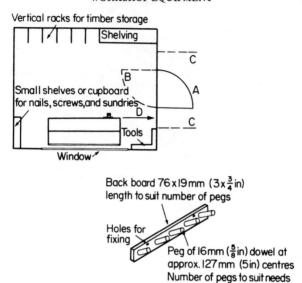

Vertical racks for timber storage

Shelving

Small shelves or cupboard for nails, screws, and sundries

Tools

Window

Back board 76 x 19 mm (3 x ¾ in) length to suit number of pegs

Holes for fixing

Peg of 16mm (⅝ in) dowel at approx. 127 mm (5 in) centres Number of pegs to suit needs

Figure 5.1. Typical home workshop (see text) and a simple tool rack

space to move around the bench from front and sides, at least, will be required.

Making a sawing stool

Before starting to make the bench something to work on, and support pieces for sawing and planing, is a requirement. The carpenter's or joiner's sawing stool, often incorrectly called a sawing horse, is a device with which we can work timber, with cramps to assist in holding if needed.

In any case the sawing stool is a handy piece of equipment to have, especially for anyone who has a lot of work to tackle around the house. It also makes a useful platform on which to stand when working at some height, and can be used in conjunction with a pair of steps to support a scaffold plank.

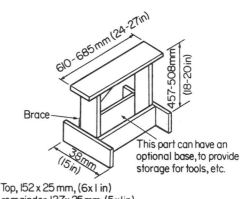

Figure 5.2. Sawing stool

The type of stool with splayed legs is not too easy for a new-comer to woodworking because of the compound angles involved in the joints. A simplified version is shown in *Figure 5.2*, where no formal joints are used and where construction relies very much on the use of screws.

Making a bench

Plans for an easy to make bench are shown in *Figure 5.3*. For a person of average height a bench with its top around 838 mm (33 in) from the floor is about right. Length can be anything from 914 mm (60 in) to 1,829 mm (72 in), but a top of about 1,524 mm (60 in) by 533 mm (21 in) gives a good working area.

The 'well' is a traditional part of the woodworker's bench; and for very good reasons. First, it provides a receptable for tools in use for any particular job and prevents them from being accidentally knocked on the floor. Secondly, wood being worked on, or jobs being assembled, can be placed across the bench without tools getting in the way. Finally, it allows the introduction of a thicker piece of wood for the front of the bench. This is the area that needs to be the most solid, partly so that the vice can be properly mounted, and also it is the front part of the bench where rigidity is most needed.

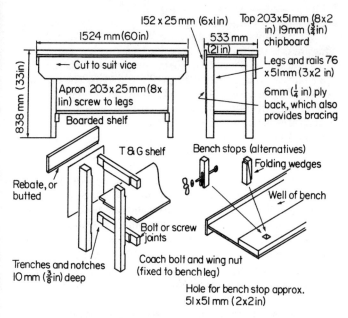

Figure 5.3. Construction of workshop bench

Legs are made from 76 × 51 mm (3 × 2 in) softwood, or 'deal', obtained from the timber merchant as P.A.R. (planed all round). Timber is measured in sawn condition — after machining it is, in fact, rather smaller than the 'nominal size'. There are also these days 'preferred sizes' and all timber is actually cut to metric dimensions within these sizes. So, the measurements of sections are more for guidance and should be taken as approximate. (For softwoods, merchants allow 25 mm as equal to an inch on sections.)

The joints for our bench are based on a simple form of trenching and notching, but without removing too much timber so as not to reduce the strength of the members. A depth of 10 mm ($\frac{3}{8}$ in) is adequate and where possible the legs and rails should be marked out in sets of four (see Chapter 3). Either a single coach bolt of 8 or 10 mm ($\frac{5}{16}$ or $\frac{3}{8}$ in) diameter can be used for fastening each joint, or the rails can be prepared for three screws at the ends. Extra strength is gained if an adhesive is used during assembly.

Chipboard or T. and G. boards can be used for the shelf, the boarding being nailed or screwed to the rails. The ply back, as well as enclosing the bench, provides a great deal of longitudinal rigidity and helps to resist the strains put on the bench, especially during planing and fairly heavy work in the vice. Ideally, the board which provides the lipping at the back should be rebated to receive the ply. The top of this lipping needs to be level with the top of the front part of the bench.

The thicker, main working area of the top of the bench should, preferably, be made of hardwood. In order both to economise and simplify construction the drawings show a variation in the usual method of forming the top. The well of the bench is made from a piece of 19 mm ($\frac{3}{4}$ in) chipboard, but with this arranged to come under the thicker front piece. The top is fixed by securing through from the upper surface but the screws need to be 'counterbored', and the resulting holes are filled with wooden dowels or 'pellets'. The chipboard must also be screwed from the underside to the thicker front member.

Bench accessories and their use

Vice

At this stage the vice should be fitted. Depending on the type and size selected, either a certain amount of recessing of the top or, alternatively, some packing will be required. *Figure 5.4* shows how a standard, Record type of vice is fixed to our bench. Detailed instructions follow at the end of the section.

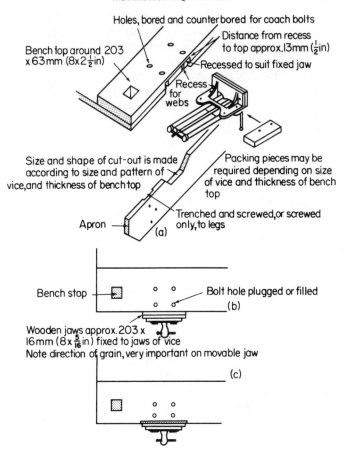

Holes, bored and counterbored for coach bolts

Bench top around 203 x 63mm (8x2½in)

Distance from recess to top approx.13mm (½in)

Recessed to suit fixed jaw

Recess for webs

Size and shape of cut-out is made according to size and pattern of vice, and thickness of benchtop

Packing pieces may be required depending on size of vice and thickness of bench top

Apron

Trenched and screwed, or screwed only, to legs

(a)

Bench stop

Bolt hole plugged or filled

(b)

Wooden jaws approx. 203 x 16mm (8x⁵⁄₁₆in) fixed to jaws of vice
Note direction of grain, very important on movable jaw

(c)

Figure 5.4. Fixing a vice to the bench

Wooden packing pieces, or 'chops', should be fixed to inner surfaces of the vice jaws before it is ready for use. The packing should be of good, solid hardwood, about 16 mm (⁵⁄₈ in) thick, preferably with the grain running vertically. The outer, movable, jaw is bored and threaded for set screws, which are used to fix the packing. The fixed jaw also has two threaded holes for engineers' machine screws, which are used to fix the inner packing. Packings are fixed level with the top of the bench and screw heads are countersunk.

The apron will have to cut around the vice, although this does not need to be a close fit. Screws are used to fix the apron to the legs, this also adding to the bracing effect needed on the bench.

Bench stop

A bench stop is essential and for this a hole is made in the bench top (*Figure 5.3*) about 51 mm (2 in) square, to coincide with the outer surface of the leg. Two forms of stop are shown: in one the stop is slotted, the vertical movement of the stop being controlled by a coach bolt and wing nut, the bolt passing through the leg and the slot fitting over it. The second pattern is simply a pair of folding wedges, easy to tighten or loosen with a tap of a hammer. Folding wedges is the term given when a pair of wedges slide together so that their outer edges remain parallel.

It is well worth while giving a new bench two or three coats of varnish. Not only does this help to keep it clean, it also means that glue which inevitably gets spilt on the top is more readily cleaned off. Finally, always ensure that the bench is standing on a level surface, and adjust the legs accordingly if necessary to make it stand firmly on all legs.

Sawing board

The most used piece of workshop equipment is a sawing board, also known as a bench hook. It is easily made from three pieces of hardwood. *Figure 5.5* shows how it is made, and approximate dimensions. Sawing boards can be made right-, left-, or dual-handed and by their simple design are double-sided.

Small chamfers should be made where indicated (A). These help to clear the sawdust which may prevent the workpiece from lying square against the board. The blocks should initially

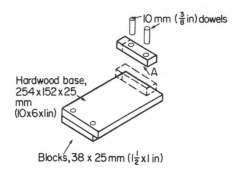

Figure 5.5. Sawing board or bench hook

be simply glued in place, then holes are bored right through and dowels are glued and pushed in, then finished off flush. Until a high standard of proficiency is reached the sawing board should be used with one block clamped in the vice.

Mitre box

A mitre box is another simple working aid which is not difficult to make (see *Figure 4.3*). Overall size is around 305 × 127 × 89 mm (12 × 5 × 3½ in), and construction is of hardwood, glued and screwed. Depth should not be greater than the sawing capacity of the tenon saw that will normally be used. Screws can be used for fixing the parts together so long as their positions are carefully made to be well clear of the saw kerfs. Kerfs should be marked out with an accurately set bevel or a mitre square. They should then carefully be cut with a tenon saw. Once made, it is virtually impossible to correct them if they are wrongly cut.

Shooting board

Chapter 3 referred to the problem of planing end grain, and the inherent risk of splitting unless precautions were taken. One of the commonest ways of tackling this problem is by using a shooting board and *Figure 5.6* shows a basic pattern.

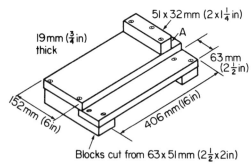

Figure 5.6. Shooting board

This is made from two pieces of 19 mm ($^3/_4$ in) hardwood or multi-ply which are screwed to supporting blocks, as shown in the drawing. Ensure that the top block is fixed exactly at right angles to the edges of the board and, in fact, make the whole assembly quite true on edges and surfaces. It also helps if the block is chamfered at corner (A) to avoid the risk of the block splitting when being used.

As drawn, the board is intended for a right-handed person. For a left-handed worker the top block should be fixed at the opposite end. Alternatively, and for dual use, blocks could be fixed at both ends but in this case the board should be made rather longer.

Cramps

When skills begin to develop and as the woodworker broadens the range of projects he/she undertakes, the need for cramps and other holding devices soon becomes apparent. These include sash cramps, G-gramps and holdfasts, and other more specialised cramps such as corner, or mitre, cramps. They are all available in a large range of sizes and are of various patterns. Patent cramping devices are now quite popular. They are cleverly designed and easy to use but the old-fashioned G-cramp still holds pride of place in most workshops.

Holdfast Frequently work needs to be held down on top of the bench as, for example, while cutting a mortise or forming a trench. For such purposes the holdfast is ideal. Such a device

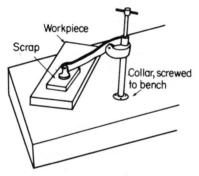

Figure 5.7. Holdfast

is shown in *Figure 5.7*. The collar is fitted into a hole drilled in the surface of the bench and housed to bring its surface flush. The collar is then screwed down. The holdfast shank is simply a sliding fit in the collar and is held by a combination of ribbed surface and friction. When the clamping arm is placed on the workpiece the turn-screw is tightened down. Combined leverage on post and clamping arm holds the work quite securely with minimum effort and time. Two collars are usually supplied with a holdfast so, with strategic positioning, quite a large area of the bench can be covered.

G-cramps   G-cramps (*Figure 5.8*) are a useful form of small cramp and have many applications in the home workshop. They too can be used to hold work on the bench and are also used on small assembly work. At one end of the available range is the 'junior' pattern — a small lightweight type in

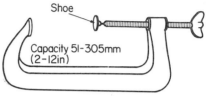

Figure 5.8. G-cramp

different capacities up to 102 mm (4 in). These are handy for toy or model making. In the middle of the range the light/ medium duty varieties can be obtained with capacities up to 305 mm (12 in). The smaller ones are fitted with wings for screwing down but the larger ones have 'tommy bars' or 'drop handles'.

The distance from the frame to the cramping screw is fairly small on most G-cramps, and this limits the distance relative to the edge at which they can operate. In practice, this is not restrictive for most applications but there is a pattern available where the throat depth is about double that of the normal type: they are known as 'deep throat cramps'.

A fairly recent innovation is the 'spring-grip' cramp. This has a small, knurled wheel let into the frame where the screw passes through. In use, the hand holding the cramp can also operate this wheel until the cramp grips sufficiently tightly to support itself, leaving the other hand free to control the work. Greater pressure can then be applied by tightening the cramp in the normal way.

Another modern variety is the edging cramp. This is a fairly small capacity cramp with a second cramping screw introduced in the centre of the frame; that is, at right angles to the main screw. Its main use is for gripping edging strips by means of the side screw once the cramp has been positioned on the work. The cramps can be used on straight or curved edges and is especially suitable for holding lippings to curved surfaces such as table tops and bookcases.

All G-cramps are fitted with swivelling shoes which automatically adjust to accommodate surfaces which are not quite parallel to each other, providing the taper is not pronounced. Scrap wood should always be used between the cramp and the work, or pressure from the screw will cause bruising. The larger the scrap, within reason, the better as this helps to spread the load. Replacement shoes are available if needed.

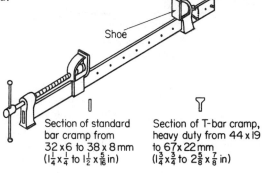

Figure 5.9. Sash cramp

Sash cramps   Sash cramps (*Figure 5.9*) are used in general assembly work and can be obtained in two main weights. The regular pattern has a bar of rectangular section, but the heavy duty pattern has a bar of T-section. The latter is intended for industrial use. Regular pattern sash cramps are available with capacities up to 1372 mm (54 in) but lengthening bars of 914 and 1219 mm (36 and 48 in) can be used with the cramps, which greatly increases the scope of the work they can tackle. It is also possible to remove the shoes from two cramps then bolt the bars together in order to increase capacity.

Always use sash cramps with considerable care as even moderate pressure wrongly applied can distort an assembly and finish up by doing more harm than good. Take, for example, two or more boards being butt or edge jointed to form a wider piece, and of a length which calls for the use of three cramps.

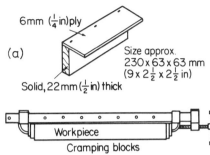

Figure 5.10. (a) Cramp packing block, (b) use of cramp packing blocks

Two of these should be placed on one side of the boards, near the ends. The third should be placed in the centre, underneath the boards. This will counteract the strain of the end cramps and keep the glued-up boards flat. If all three cramps are placed on the top side the boards will probably bow as pressure is applied.

When a frame is properly assembled and checked it must be correctly left for the glue to set and the work to dry out. This means that the cramped up job should be left on a flat surface for several hours or, if left in a vertical position, checked that it is not under strain from its own weight.

As with all cramps, packing of some sort must be introduced between cramp jaws and the work. It is also desirable to have scrap between the bar of the cramp and the assembly. This eliminates the risk of any part of the cramp causing damage to the work. It also prevents spoiling from a less obvious source. It is normal practice to wash off any surplus glue when the job is in cramps. This often results in the work being wetted. If a cramp is in contact with damp wood a pronounced stain can be the result. This can be difficult to remove and the lighter the wood the more obstinate becomes the stain.

As an aid to cramping, simple cramp packing blocks can be

made. These are glued and pinned together as shown in *Figure 5.10 (a)*. In use, the thicker part is positioned under the shoe of the cramp (*b*).

Cramp heads   Perhaps one of the most useful forms of cramp for the amateur is one which is partly home-made, using what are called 'cramp heads' (*Figure 5.11*). These are, in effect, the

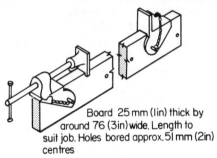

Board 25 mm (1in) thick by around 76 (3in) wide. Length to suit job. Holes bored approx. 51 mm (2in) centres

Figure 5.11. Cramp heads

two working ends of a sash cramp, without the bar. The heads are used in conjunction with a wooden bar 25 mm (1 in) thick, which forms the bar part of the cramp. One big advantage of cramp heads is that cramps of considerable length can be made. Width of the wooden bar should be about 63 to 102 mm ($2\frac{1}{2}$ to 3 in), depending on length but hardwood bars up to about 1220 mm (4 ft) need only be 101 mm (2 in) wide. For the sliding shoe, holes for the fixing pin should be made about 101 mm (2 in) apart.

Corner cramp   A rather more specialised form of cramp is the corner cramp. This has two threaded screws mounted at 90° to one another, applying pressure against a right-angled fence. The two mitred pieces of wood forming the corner (angle of a picture frame, for instance) are gripped under respective pressure screws and are held accurately in relation to each other. There are several variations of this type of cramp.

Fixing a standard vice to the bench

Two main dimensions are to be considered in connection with vices: width of jaws or size of clamping face, and distance between the jaws when they are fully opened.

The smallest vice of any real, but limited, use has a jaw width of 152 mm (6 in) opening to 114 mm ($4\frac{1}{2}$ in). This size is also available with a built-in clamp on the underside, enabling it to be fastened to the top of a bench or table.

For the more serious worker a heavier vice should be considered. Such vices are more robustly made, have a deeper capacity from top of jaws down to slides and screws and also open wider. Although there are many sizes, one with 178 mm (7 in) wide jaws opening to 203 mm (8 in) should be adequate for most home undertakings.

This range of vices offers alternative types of screw action. One is a plain screw which has to be turned until the required opening is reached; the other is known as a 'quick action screw'. With this one there is a small lever at the front, near the screw head. When this is depressed the screw is disengaged from the fixed jaw and the movable jaw slides back or forward. When released, the normal clamping action can be made by turning the screw. This is a great time saver when there is a lot of working with the vice. Mounting sequences when fixing such vices are similar in each case.

A medium size vice, such as the 7 in one previously described, is suitable for the bench illustrated in *Figure 5.3*. In *Figure 5.4* we show fixing details for the popular Record pattern vice. The vice should be fitted carefully and rigidly anchored.

The front edge of the bench will need a certain amount of recessing to accommodate the fixed jaw and the two webs which add strength to the frame (*a*). The size and extent of this recess will depend on two main factors: the thickness of the top is the first. A vice should be fixed so that the top of the jaws is about 13 mm ($\frac{1}{2}$ in) below the top surface of the bench. The main reason for this is to keep the metal of the vice well clear of tools being used on work held by the vice. Chisels, saws and planes can easily be blunted or damaged by accidental contact with the metal.

Secondly, the way in which the wooden jaws are attached to the metal ones must be considered. Wooden jaws must always be added to a woodworker's vice, mainly to protect the work. Without this precaution the metal will surely bruise or mark any wooden parts gripped in the vice.

Alternative ways of fixing the jaw faces are shown in *Figure 5.4* at (b) and (c). In method (b) the fixed jaw projects beyond the edge of the bench, but at (c) it is flush. Some craftsmen prefer one way while some prefer the other, as each has its merits. For instance, the vice at (b) will often cope more easily with partly assembled work while (c) is better when planing the edge of a long board because a certain amount of lateral support is offered by the whole length of the edge of the bench top.

In method (b) the depth of the recess must be equal to the thickness of the metal fixed jaw. In (c) it must be equal to the thickness of the metal plus the thickness of the wooden face — around 16 to 18 mm ($^5/_8$ to $^3/_4$ in). The recess would then need to be extended beyond the edges of the metal jaws to allow for the wooden facing, and this usually has its ends dovetailed into the bench, as shown.

For smaller vices coach screws could be used for securing the vice. They are, of course, driven in from the underside, and are in no way visible from the top. With larger vices and for maximum security coach bolts are better. Although engineers' types of bolts could be used coach bolts, with their large head and square shank immediately under the head are intended specially for use with wood. The heads, however, must be let into the top of the bench. Holes prepared in this way are known as 'counterbored'. Washers should always be used under the nut. Holes in the top should be filled once the bolts are tightened. This can be done either by gluing in dowels of wood or by using a proprietary filler.

Where a fairly large vice is being added to a bench with a relatively thin top, it might well be that packing will have to be introduced between the underside of the bench and the vice. This is to compensate for the thickness of the top so that the jaws of the vice when fixed will be below the top surface, as before explained. *Figure 5.4 (a)* shows one of the two packing pieces which may be needed. The actual thickness of these pieces would, of course, depend on the factors described.

The apron piece will require a certain amount of shaping. This, however, does not have to be precise as there is no need for the apron to be a tight fit around the vice. The exact shape and extent of this shaping will depend on the thickness of the bench top, and the size of the vice. Apron and bench top are usually arranged so that the top overhangs the apron by about 16 to 18 mm ($\frac{5}{8}$ to $\frac{3}{4}$ in). This overhang would then determine the thickness of the wooden faces used in (*b*).

The jaws should be made of hardwood as this best resists the wear to which they are subjected. It is very important that the grain on the moving jaw is vertical: if it is horizontal then the part projecting above the metal can easily split when something is held right at the top of the vice, and the vice is then well tightened.

On most vices the metal jaws are drilled and tapped to accept 'set screws' for fixing the wooden faces. It is, however, possible to use ordinary wood screws from the back of the jaw, into the wood. Set screws pass through holes drilled in the wood faces, and make a much stronger fixing. Whichever way they are fixed care must be taken to ensure that the inner faces of the wood jaws are left smooth and without screw heads that stand proud, or screw points sticking through. The wooden jaws need replacing from time to time and care must always be taken in their fitting so that when the vice is closed the surfaces of the wood remain parallel both vertically and horizontally.

Do not grip metal objects in the wooden faces and take care of the vice, with an occasional drop of oil on slide and screws. When gripping irregular shaped material be sure to place soft-wood packing pieces at the 'slack' spots so that the pressure is evenly exerted.

6 Portable Power Tools

One of the many changes which have taken place in recent years is the development of small portable power tools for home workers. Woodworking is well catered for, although the tools are not as robust or powerful as their industrial counterparts. The power source is always domestic mains electricity and the tools are as portable as the availability of a power outlet and the length of lead on the tool or added as an extension.

A safety point to stress right away is that extension leads on reels should be fully opened out when used for more than a few minutes, otherwise the wound up cable overheats to an extent which may burn out the insulation.

The power drill and its attachments

Most of the popular power drills have many attachments or accessories available for them, which either fit in the chuck or can be attached to the drive after the chuck has been removed. In general terms an attachment means that the chuck has to be removed − a simple operation − while an accessory fits the chuck. With these, the power drill owner can convert a single tool into a multi-purpose piece of equipment.

Drill sizes and types

The smallest and cheapest drill on the market has a chuck capacity of 6 mm ($\frac{1}{4}$ in). This means that the shank of drill or other accessory being fitted cannot exceed that size. Also explicit in the specification is the warning that attempting to drill in metal over 6 mm diameter will seriously overload the machine and probably destroy it.

This type of drill has a speed of around 2 500 revolutions per minute (r.p.m.) when running free, or unloaded. When the drill is actually under load, or working, the speed will drop. As the load is increased the motor will begin to labour and heat up rapidly until 'stalling' point is reached. Long before this stage is reached the user should have reduced the load.

Chuck capacity and no-load speed are standard specifications for power drills. The speed quoted is quite satisfactory for boring small diameter holes in wood but it is too fast for drilling in steel or masonry. Power output of the motors fitted in these small drills varies from maker to maker but typical working capacities are 6 mm diameter holes in steel and 13 mm ($\frac{1}{2}$ in) in hardwoods.

A very popular drill for home use is one with a chuck capacity of 10 mm ($\frac{3}{8}$ in). The power is uprated above the smaller capacity drill and the 10 mm drill should be able to drill in steel up to 10 mm diameter and 19 mm ($\frac{3}{4}$ in) in wood. With this capacity of drill variations are available in no-load speeds. The first is a two-speed model providing a fast speed suitable for wood and a slower speed intended for drilling in steel or masonry. Typical speeds are around 3 000 r.p.m. and 700/850 r.p.m.

The problem of drill speed and the need to have fast and slow revolutions has been overcome by some manufacturers with various electronic circuits which reduce the current flowing to the motor, thus reducing its speed. Some infinitely variable speed drills can run from only a few revolutions a minute up to maximum by trigger control only, the trigger acting rather like an accelerator.

Speed-changing accessories

Other devices to change the speed of a drill are available as accessories. One is in the form of a secondary chuck which fits into the drill chuck. It is, in principle, a small gear box which reduces the speed by about half. Some patterns can be reversed, thus increasing the speed, while others are arranged so that the drilling is done at right angles to the machine's axis. This arrangement can on occasions be quite useful in awkward or constrained situations.

Another piece of equipment which can be used to vary the speed of a drill is in the form of an electronic variable control which is plugged in line with the drill lead. By operating a knob the speed can be reduced from maximum to minimum, within the control design. The principles on which these gadgets work are, broadly, rapid interruption of the current flow which in effect switches the drill off and on again; makers claim that this system, whether plugged in line or built into the drill itself, does not reduce the torque, or turning power, of the tool.

Drill stands

For most of the time a drill is used it is hand-held and used free-hand. Indeed, for many drilling operations this is the only way it can be used. There are, however, many occasions when a drill becomes far more efficient and easier to use when it is clamped in a drill stand. Repetition work and when drilling metals are two examples of when a drill is more efficient when in a stand. Most leading manufacturers make stands for their own drills and some make stands which will accept other makes of drill. In the domestic range one, at least, makes a stand for drilling which also forms part of a small wood-turning lathe, powered by the drill. There is a certain amount of interchangeability between drills and stands of various makers but this should be checked before purchase.

A drill stand should be robust and smooth in action, with no backlash in the linkages. For safety it should be bolted or screwed to a suitable bench. If this is not practicable it should, at least, be clamped or otherwise secured to the work bench or table.

Mortising bits and attachments

Not only do stands make drilling operations easier to perform, they also open up the way for further attachments to be used. The bigger and stronger stands can be equipped to make mortises, using the very efficient hollow, square mortising chisels and bits, sold by good tools shops (*Figure 6.1*).

This type of tool has a special bit which revolves in the hollow centre of the chisel. When the chisel is pressed down

Figure 6.1. Hollow square mortise chisel and bit

on the wood the bit bores a hole, ejecting the waste through a hole in the top of the chisel, which continues the cut, converting the round hole to a square one. By taking a series of cuts side by side a mortise of any length can be made. For the most satisfactory cutting of mortises, the chisel should equal the width of the mortise.

Because of the limitations inherent in this system, the largest bit which can be used is $\frac{1}{2}$ in. These chisels are not made by the firms who supply the drills but by specialist firms. A leading firm supplies them in five sizes, from $\frac{1}{4}$ to $\frac{1}{2}$ in, but not as yet in metric sizes.

Shaper cutters

A recent development in power tool attachments is the shaper cutter, which fits directly in the chuck. A range of cutters allows cuts such as beading, chamfering, coving, rounding, grooving and rebating to be made, as in *Figure 6.2*. They can

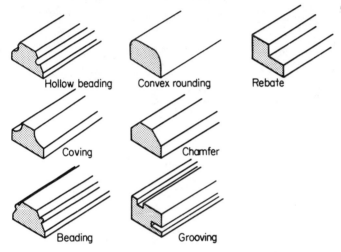

Hollow beading   Convex rounding   Rebate

Coving   Chamfer

Beading   Grooving

Figure 6.2. Cuts which can be made using a shaper cutter

be used in conjunction with a drill stand or in a hand shaper attachment (*Figure 6.3*). One supplier of these cutters produces a universal shaper table, designed for fitting to popular drill stands and providing a fixed work table with an adjustable fence (*Figure 6.4*). The table fits on to the base of the drill stand.

With a slotting type cutter a groove the width of the cutter can be made, or by repeating the cut after some adjustment to the fence a wider groove can be made. This can be repeated to form quite wide grooves. By grooving from two adjacent faces, rebates can also be made.

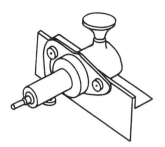

Figure 6.3. Hand shaper attachment

Adjustable fence

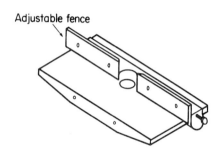

Figure 6.4. Shaper table

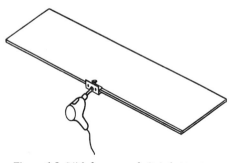

Figure 6.5. With large panels it is better to use the hand shaper, rather than move the wood across the shaper table

The hand shaper attachment performs the same function as the shaper table but, whereas the drill is fixed with the table to the drill stand and the wood moves across the cutter, with the shaper attachment the drill and cutter move across the wood, which is usually held in a vice, or clamped to the bench. The hand attachment is particularly suitable when making a cut in a fairly large piece of wood, as in *Figure 6.5*. It would be far more difficult to move such a piece across the small table in a drill stand than to move the attachment along the timber.

Circular saws

Circular saw attachments for power drills can be used for many jobs, especially ripping and cutting man-made boards. They have blades up to approximately 127 mm (5 in) diameter and can be used at the place of work, with an extension lead plugged in at a convenient socket outlet. The saws are easily attached to the drill and have adjustable depth and angle of cut. The blade is enclosed by a guard when not actually cutting and the guard snaps closed by a light spring when the saw finishes its cut.

Most saws have a ripping fence which can be adjusted to about 300 mm (6 in) from the face and the fence can be removed as required. The sole plate of the saw has a cut-out section at the leading edge of the blade so the operator can see the line of cut and many have a guide line on the sole plate to assist the lead-in to the cutting line.

Saw bench

A small saw bench to which the circular saw attachment can be mounted further increases the scope of a power drill (*Figure 6.6*). The attachment, with the drill, is mounted under or on top of the bench (according to make) with the blade protruding through the table top. Maximum depth of cut is about 38 mm ($1\frac{1}{2}$ in) but thicker material can be ripped by first grooving then turning the timber over and completing the cut. The work should not be forced through the saw, just lightly thrust against the revolving blade and pressed firmly against fence and table.

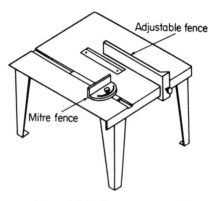

Figure 6.6. Multi-purpose saw table

The ripping fence is adjustable and frequently a mitre and cutting-off fence is provided. This slides in a groove as shown in the diagram, transporting the workpiece through the saw.

Circular saw blades

Most circular saw attachments are supplied with a 'general purpose' blade (*Figure 6.7*). This has coarse teeth of the rip saw profile, for cutting along the grain. Tips of the teeth, however, are sharpened with side bevels as shown, so that the outer tips of the teeth cut first. This is a requirement for cross-cutting as it helps to prevent the grain from splitting on the underside of the wood.

The blade can therefore be used for most wood-cutting functions, but has slight drawbacks. The teeth are quite large and tend to tear the grain, especially on thin sections.

Smaller teeth give a cleaner finish and absorb less power from the drill; the power of the motor tends to govern the speed of the cut, rather than tooth size. Fine teeth blades, as shown in *Figure 6.8 (a)*, are available and should be used for sawing plywood or hardboard or thin sections of timber.

For the person who expects to do a lot of sawing, a tungsten carbide tipped (T.C.T.) blade (*b*) is a worthwhile investment.

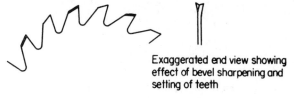

Exaggerated end view showing effect of bevel sharpening and setting of teeth

Figure 6.7. General purpose blade – ripsaw shape teeth but with tips 'bevel' sharpened

(a)   (b)

Figure 6.8. A saw with smaller teeth will give a much smoother finish

These blades are relatively expensive but have a life between sharpenings of fifty times or more greater than an ordinary steel blade. They also leave a much smoother cut surface. Home users cannot, however, re-sharpen them, and they must be sent to a specialist for servicing.

Jig saw

Another saw attachment available for many makes of drill is the jig saw. This has a short, narrow blade with which curves and awkward shapes can be cut. The blade reciprocates in an up and down movement, with the teeth so shaped that it cuts on the upward stroke. These saws cut quite well on thinner material but the rate of cutting can become rather slow on wood near the saw's maximum capacity, usually 19 mm ($^3/_4$ in).

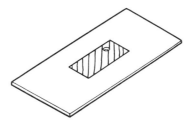

Figure 6.9. Hole bored in waste so that jig saw blade can be inserted

A jig saw is particularly useful when it is required to cut a hole of some sort from the centre of a panel or board. A hole may be needed to introduce the saw (*Figure 6.9*), but with some types of jig saw they will 'work themselves in'. How this can be done is explained in the instruction leaflet.

Woodturning lathe

Mention has already been made of a drill-powered lathe. A woodturning lathe is usually a fairly heavy and robust type of machine, so it may be realised that those which are basically power drill attachments are very much in the lightweight class. In spite of this they are capable of producing satisfactory work so long as it is accepted that they have limitations and that only fairly small work can be turned on them.

Lathes of this type will turn work up to about 457–508 mm (18–20 in) in length and 100 mm (2 in) in diameter. The length of work possible is referred to as 'between centres' capacity. They will cope with face-plate jobs (bowls, plates, etc.) up to about 102 mm (4 in) diameter.

For the beginner who wants to start off on woodturning, there are sets of woodturning tools below the size normally used on standard lathes. A recommended set, made by one of the best known tool manufacturers, comprises three principal tools in the small-size range: a 13 mm (½ in) gouge, same size skew chisel, and a parting tool.

Grindstones

The cradle which holds the power drill, forming the headstock of the lathe, can be used for other purposes. One is to enable the drill to be used to turn a small grindstone. The maximum size of stone which can be mounted on the drill is about 127 mm (5 in) diameter, by 13 mm ($\frac{1}{2}$ in) thick. It is used in conjunction with a special mandrel, or arbor, on which the stone is mounted at one end, the other going directly into the drill chuck.

Disc sanders

One of the most simple attachments is the disc sander. This is a circular, flexible rubber pad of 127 to 152 mm (5 to 6 in) diameter, mounted on a small arbor. The shank fits chucks of $\frac{1}{4}$ in capacity upwards. A disc of abrasive paper is held by a screw in the centre of the pad, which is dished to keep the screw below the working surface. When in use the outer edge of the disc is lightly kept in contact with the work and constantly on the move – the abrasive action is quite effective, especially if a coarse one is being used.

Because of the circular action much of the sanding is across the grain. As a result, there is a tendency to scratch the surface, leaving circular marks. Because of this the disc sander is only really suitable for work which is to be painted, when slight surface scratches will be obliterated, or when trimming across end grain, edges of plywood and hardboard, or 'fairing off' when boatbuilding.

Abrasive discs

As well as the traditional abrasive paper, other abrasive discs can be obtained which, it is claimed, have certain advantages over the paper. One of these is a thin metal disc, shaped and dished to fit the rubber backing pads. At a stage in the manufacture small particles of tungsten carbide are bonded to the surface. Because of the extreme hardness of the abrasive granules, a very long life is claimed.

Another type of disc is in the form of resin-bonded matting, woven from abrasive-impregnated materials. Although the disc itself is rather stiff the weave is 'open', thus allowing dust to pass through. This means that the disc does not clog up, which is one of the problems of ordinary abrasive papers.

Orbital sanders

A much more gentle abrasive action is achieved with an orbital or finishing sander, also available as a drill attachment. Used correctly and with a fine abrasive sheet, the finishing sander produces a smooth matt surface which is used extensively on modern furniture. With coarse grits, orbital sanders can be used to rub down paintwork but they are not intended to clean off rough or sawn surfaces.

Drill bits

Many other attachments and accessories, not necessarily for woodworking, are available for power drills and, with such a wide range available, it is easy to overlook what the power drill is primarily designed for: to bore holes.

In order to bore holes properly and precisely, the correct type of bit must be used. Bits intended for holding in a carpenter's brace cannot be used as they have square, thick, shanks which cannot be gripped in the power drill chuck.

The most common type of bit used in the power drill is the engineers' pattern, shown in *Figure 6.10 (a)*. There are different qualities of this type — the cheapest are referred to as 'jobbers' quality', suitable for occasional use in soft materials. These drills do not like a high speed and if used in a single (high speed) power drill to bore in metals, they will quickly lose the cutting edge and stop drilling. Jobbers' drills are not made to a high degree of accuracy but they are close enough in tolerances for wood.

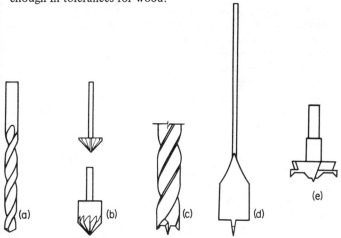

Figure 6.10. Power drill bits: (a) engineer's twist drill, (b) countersinks, (c) lip and spur, (d) flat bit, (e) 'end mill', for use with concealed hinges

A rather better type of drill is made from carbon steel. They also do not like high speeds when drilling metal — especially steel — but are unaffected when drilling wood. High speed when drilling a hard material causes friction, and this in turn creates heat. Only a slight excess of heat is enough to draw the cutting edge temper and once this is lost friction and heat build up until the drill tip turns blue and is useless. Sharpness of drill, slow speed and moderate pressure are essential when using carbon drills.

The best type is the high-speed drill. These can be run at high speed without damage, and with sensible care will give many years of service. Engineers' drills are available in metric and imperial sizes, and also in a 'letter' range. For woodworking purposes these drills are ideal for boring the sort of holes needed for screws, when it is important that the holes should be just the right size to match the gauge of screws. The drills are also useful for drilling pilot holes when using large nails and it is desirable to pre-drill to prevent splitting the wood.

When fixing a drill bit in the chuck (and, indeed, when fitting any attachment or accessory to a drill) first be sure that the drill is disconnected from the power supply. Then check that the bit is properly centred in the chuck before tightening up with the chuck key, usually a lever device which plugs into holes bored in the chuck body. A small toothed wheel engages with similar teeth cut around the chuck. When the chuck is sufficiently tight fit the lever in the next hole and tighten again. Do this in all the holes (usually three). This ensures that the bit is truly central and secure.

Many domestic woodworking jobs involve fixing pieces of wood to the walls. This means drilling and plugging the wall for screws; a power drill with the correct type of boring bit will make quick work of a job which, by hand, would take many times as long and would be extremely tiring.

A masonry drill is essential. Such drills are numbered to match plug and screw sizes, and it is important that they do match for many reasons. These drills must not be driven at a high speed, which leads to overheating but they should have a moderate amount of pressure. Too little pressure means that the tip rubs, rather than cuts.

Although a tipped masonry drill will retain its cutting edge for a good while when properly used, it needs to be sharpened from time to time. For this purpose a special grinding wheel is needed. Tungsten carbide is too hard to be sharpened on an ordinary grindstone or oilstone. For tipped drills the stone to use is known as a 'green grit', and it operates without creating sparks. These drills, however, are best left to specialist firms, unless one wishes to experiment with the smaller, cheaper sizes.

All engineers' drills can be re-sharpened on an ordinary

grindstone, smooth or medium grit. It is essential to retain the original angles and shapes and this can be achieved with a little practice. There are special grinding jigs and machines for 'touching up' engineers' drills and they do not cost a lot.

When holes are made for screws it may be necessary to countersink for the screw head. There are two popular patterns of countersink bit for power drills, as shown in *Figure 6.10 (b)*, but there is nothing to choose between them in their perform-ance. It is always better to slightly over-countersink to ensure that the screw head does not lie above the surface. Sometimes the countersinking is made deliberately excessive so that the head of the screw can be concealed by filling with 'stopping'.

A very efficient bit for boring wood is known as the 'lip and spur', shown in *Figure 6.10 (c)*. These bits have a small central point, slightly longer than the cutter spurs, which are characteristic of many patterns of wood-boring bits. They are made in many sizes up to 25 mm (1 in) but with 6 mm ($\frac{1}{4}$ in) shanks on the smaller sizes and 13 mm ($\frac{1}{2}$ in) on the larger. These bits are excellent for boring holes of the size and type used when making dowel joints.

For the home woodworker, flatbits (*d*) are the cheapest for use in power drills. They are very simply made and were developed especially for portable power drills. They have a large point on which the flat cutting part rotates – the two cutting edges, in fact, scrape rather than cut. Despite this they bore quickly in wood and sharpening is easy, using a fine file. The bits are available up to 38 mm ($1\frac{1}{2}$ in) in diameter and all have 6 mm ($\frac{1}{4}$ in) shanks. Although they absorb little power the largest of these bits may be too much for the cheaper drills with 6 mm chucks.

More specialised bits, which can only be satisfactorily used when the drill is in a stand, include the screw Jennings pattern, the Forstner pattern, and the saw-tooth centre bit. The first two are similar to those used in a carpenter's brace, excepting the shank. Special bits, sometimes called end mills, are now made for machine-boring the holes for 'concealed' hinges used extensively on modern furniture (*e*).

Single purpose or integral machines

Excellent though most attachments are, they do not perform quite as well, or have the same capacity, as a power tool designed for a single function. With an independent machine power and speed are matched for optimum performance, and this can never be achieved in quite the right balance with a single power source.

Separate, or integral, machines are easier to use, often requiring only one hand compared with two for the equivalent attachment. The range of independent machines is very wide and covers a great many woodworking operations.

Orbital, dual motion and belt sanders

Sanders are possibly among the more popular in this range of integral machines. Most are of the type called 'orbital' because of the circular motion which the rectangular sanding pad makes. The amount of wood they are capable of removing is only slight, therefore a surface should be in a reasonable state before this type of sander is used.

There are some sanders on the market which are classed as 'dual-motion'. They can operate as a normal orbital sander or, by moving a small lever, the movement changes to a straight up-and-down, or in-line action. This means that the sanding can always be arranged to be with the grain – an orbital movement is bound to have part of the stroke across the grain. However, because of the nature of this machine, the extent of swirl-scratching is only slight. The in-line sander does not produce a matt surface, as the orbital one does, so the dual motion sander at least gives a choice of finish.

By far the best type of portable sander is the belt sander. The abrasive is an endless belt about 102 mm (4 in) or more in width. The machines are usually designed so that on one side the belt extends beyond the body, thus allowing the sanding to take place right up to the edges. Belt sanders are capable of moving quite a lot of wood fairly quickly, and because of this the bigger and more powerful machines are fitted with dust bags or dust extraction systems. Cutting action is in one direction only and wherever possible this should be arranged to be with the grain. Belt sanders are very effective but their cost is many times that of an orbital sander.

Abrasives

Machine type abrasive paper or cloth must be used in all power sanders. This is normally bought to suit the size and type of machine for which it is needed. The grit is nearly always aluminium oxide and, although a wide range of grades is manufactured, popular packs are often available in assorted sizes: coarse, medium and fine.

When used on wood which is resinous, there is often a tendency for the paper to stop cutting because clogged with resin and dust, rather than normal wear. A rub with a wire brush will usually clear the surface, and extend the life of the abrasive paper considerably.

Jigsaws

The jigsaw machine is available as a single- or two-speed tool. As with boring holes, a fast speed is needed for wood and a slow speed for metal. Blades have a limited life but are quite cheap and quickly changed, being held in place by a set screw or on some makes, two screws. Various types of blade can be fitted, large or small teeth for cutting wood and very small teeth for metals. Because of the upward cutting action, sawdust is deposited on top of the work, right on the cutting line. Many of the better jigsaws have built-in blowers to clear the dust from the line.

When a hole has to be cut in the centre of a panel, it is necessary to bore a hole in the centre of the panel to 'start' the saw. It is advisable to bore holes at all sharp angles, the diameter equalling the width of the saw blade. Although jigsaws (sometimes also called sabre-saws) are particularly suited to cutting holes inside panels, and for cutting shaped pieces, they can also be used for straight cutting. Some makers provide a guide fence which can be fitted to the sole plate, for sawing parallel to an edge. It is not likely that the fence can

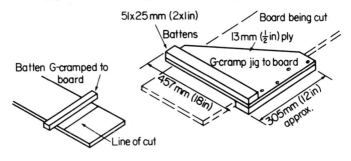

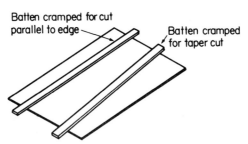

Figure 6.11. Cutting guides for use with jigsaw machines or circular saws

be used for cross-cutting or for cuts well away from the edge but a batten can be temporarily fixed to the board and this used to guide the saw. It is also possible to make a simple jig which can be G-cramped to the board and thus give an accurate, square cut every time. Some ideas and suggestions for cutting guides are shown in *Figure 6.11*. They can also be used for circular saws.

Portable power saws

Portable power saws are capable of quite heavy cutting. Blade sizes range from around 152 mm (5 in) to 229 mm (9 in). A popular size is about 190 mm ($7\frac{1}{2}$ in) and this machine will cut timber up to 63 mm ($2\frac{1}{2}$ in) in one pass. Most of the saws are fitted with a safety clutch which automatically stops the blade from revolving if the motor is being overloaded. In the interests of safety the trigger is spring loaded and returned to 'off' if released. A retractable blade guard is fitted which uncovers the blade as it works into the wood and returns as the saw clears from the cut or the wood.

A fence can be fitted to the sole plate, enabling cuts to be made parallel with an edge. When the cut is at a distance from the edge greater than the operating capacity of the fence then guides or jigs can be used, as in *Figure 6.11*.

Grindstones and their use

Machine driven grindstones are useful in a busy workshop. Small ones are in two main sizes: 127 mm (5 in) diameter by 13 mm ($\frac{1}{2}$ in) thick, and 152 × 25 mm (6 in × 1 in). Most of the machines are double-ended, enabling different grades of wheels to be mounted. Those usually fitted as standard are medium and fine; adjustable tool rests and guards are now a standard requirement on grindstones, with eye shields. If the grindstone does not have eye shields then safety glasses or goggles should be worn when using the machine.

These grinders will cope very adequately with all the general requirements of home and workshop. When grinding cutting tools on these 'dry' grindstones there is the risk of overheating the cutting edge and 'drawing the temper'. This means that the metal in the cutting edge has changed its characteristics and will not retain its cutting edge when used. If the heating becomes excessive the end of the blade turns blue or purple. This burnt area would then have to be ground away to reach unspoilt cutting steel.

Two main points need watching in order to prevent this overheating from taking place. One is to use only gentle pressure. Too much pressure, in a bid to speed up the grinding, creates excessive friction and heat. Secondly, keep a container of water handy so that every few seconds the tool can be dipped in the water to cool it. Many grinders have a container or trough attached to them for this purpose. Although the motors are usually well protected, do not splash water over them — water and electricity are a dangerous combination.

Other precautions are: keep the tool on the move as far as this is possible, and ensure that the grindstone itself is cutting properly. Wheel dressers can be purchased for truing up and resurfacing grindstones.

Bandsaws

Mention should be made of bandsaws. There are some on the market which are portable in the sense that they can be carried to the working area. A bandsaw is a fine, versatile machine which does require careful and considerate handling. After some practice the operation of a bandsaw should present no difficulties and such a tool is worth considering when skills and requirements develop.

Do's and don't's for power tools

All machine tools have an element of danger in their handling and use. Correct wiring up is the first safety check to make. Proper earthing of most tools is essential but an exception is tools classed as 'double insulated'.

We have already warned about having a drill connected to the power source while fitting attachments or accessories. Other 'do's and don't's now follow.

DO learn to understand the tool, what it can tackle, and also its limitations. Read and apply the information given in the instruction booklet.

DO NOT experiment with it or try to perform functions for which it is not designed.

DO keep the guards and safety devices fully operational.

DO NOT tie them back out of the way or jamb them with a match stick or nail.

DO maintain tidy habits, and keep the work area well lit, clear and clean.

DO NOT work in your own light.

DO store tools properly when not in use. Keep them out of the reach of children.

DO NOT allow children to get too close. They are naturally curious but do not appreciate potential danger.

DO use the correct tool for the job.

DO NOT force tools. Experience soon shows at which speed the tool performs best, this being the speed for which it was designed.

DO hold the workpiece firmly with cramps or in a vice. Keep hands away from moving parts.

DO NOT adjust or service a machine with the power supply on — always disconnect.

DO keep tools in good working order. Blunt tools can be dangerous — cutting edges must be kept sharp.

DO NOT put them away while dirty or wet. Clean them up properly.

DO switch off the power source, or disconnect tools when not in use.

DO NOT leave power tools switched on when unplugged from the power supply. This could lead to accidental starting when plugging in again.

DO make sure that chuck keys and other tightening devices are removed before switching on.

DO NOT leave them lying around on the bench or in the workshop but tie or clip them to the machine power lead.

DO be most careful when a machine has been switched off and is being put down. It is very easy to catch the cable or something while the drive is still revolving.

DO NOT place it where it can be knocked off or tripped over.

DO ensure that when extension leads are used they are positioned where they will not be damaged or tripped over.

DO NOT leave a lot of spare cable wound on a reel — open it out but place it tidily.

DO be tidy in your dress. Loose ties and cuffs can easily be caught in moving parts.

DO NOT scorn overalls or protective clothing.

7 Finishing Processes

The terms 'finish' and 'finishing process' have a particular meaning when applied to woodwork and refer to the way in which surfaces are treated. This is usually by the application of a liquid coating material which dries by evaporation of solvents and/or oxidisation of the vehicle in which the constituents are suspended. Reasons for applying a finish are many. They include: preventing (or at least retarding) decay, as in fencing; protecting the woodwork from the elements; introducing bright and attractive colours; protecting the wood surface from wear and abrasion, chemical attack and so on; and enhancing the natural beauty of the wood, which is the aim of a cabinet maker. Finishes also protect the wood surface from dirt, spillages and many other hazards in the domestic and commercial spheres. Where mixed species of wood have been used on a single project the finish selected may be to highlight the colour differences, or to try to bring the mixed woods to a uniform shade.

Preparation for finishing, known as 'cleaning up', has been described previously but it will vary according to the nature of the job and the type of finish to be applied. At one extreme, timber that has to be creosoted will not require any preparation other than ensuring that it is reasonably dry. At the other end of the scale a finely made piece of furniture will require very careful and thorough cleaning up as a preparation for applying the finish, with or without staining.

Finishes for woodwork come under two main categories: opaque and clear. Paints of various kinds provide the main types of opaque finishes, which include oil, vinyl, emulsion, cellulose-based and enamels. Generally the type of paint is determined by the liquid vehicle, or solvent (thinner) used in the manufacture.

Clear finishes include wax, oil, shellac, white french polish, varnish, clear cellulose and modern 'plastic' finishes.

It should be understood that while paints have an obliterating effect they do not make up for poor work or shoddy materials. The quality of a painted finish depends partly on the paint itself, and to a much greater extent on the surface to which it is applied. A poorly cleaned up or ill-prepared surface will show through the best of paint. Small blemishes, if carefully filled, stopped and levelled off, properly treated knots and other minor faults, nail and screw holes, can become undetectable under a carefully applied paint.

If a clear finish is required, whether stain will be used or not, then the surface needs even more preparation. A commonly held belief is that any form of finish covers up faults in materials or workmanship. Not only is this wrong but the opposite is actually true. Clear finishes have the effect of highlighting and magnifying defects. The slightest of ridges, which insufficient glass-papering has failed to remove, may be difficult to spot before finishing but can become very noticeable afterwards. By then it is too late to do anything about it.

Preparation for the finish, following the cleaning up process described in an earlier section, includes stopping, filling and staining.

Stopping and filling

Stopping means filling cracks, holes and indentations with a plastic material which dries fairly quickly and adheres firmly. There are many preparations available in powder or paste form. The powders are mixed with water, and pastes are applied as they are supplied. Ideally the stopper should have the same density and porosity when dry as the surface being treated. It is an advantage also if it is of the same colour, but this is of less importance with painted finishes.

Although used extensively at one time, linseed oil putty is not a good stopper. It is slow drying, eventually shrinks and does not have good adhesion. Plaster of paris expands some time after it has set and causes 'blowing'.

Cellulose type stoppings are inert and have good adhesion. They are quite good for preparing wood that has to be painted, but as they are water-mixed they dry slowly. Resin putties are quick drying and special ones for wood are excellent, but not readily available in the domestic market.

The author has used powder stopping mixed with resin into a putty-like paste, then added the catalyst or hardener and used the paste as a stopping for exterior woodwork, with excellent results, including rapid setting. Even car body repair resin paste will make a good and quick-drying stopper, although rather expensive, for painted wood that has suffered some damage.

For varnishing and polishing, open grain needs to be filled. As with stoppings, many types are available, ready mixed or in powder form.

Grain fillers are rubbed in with a damp rag, across the grain. When dry, as with stopping, they are sanded smooth. If required, a further application is made until a satisfactory surface is achieved.

The filler should be near enough the colour of the wood, but light coloured fillers can often be toned down with water-based stains such as Furniglas, even if the woodwork itself is going to be stained during the next stage of work.

Various tools are used to apply stoppings and fillers — a painter's broad-knife is useful — but often enough a wood chisel makes a good applicator for dealing with small holes. The materials can also be scraped on with strips of plastics sheet, scraps of plywood, card etc.

Brushes

Quality of tools and materials used for finishing is important. It is always better to play safe and use the products of a reliable manufacturer. This applies particularly to brushes, where the cheaper 'household' types should be avoided. When buying, choose a brush which has long bristles, and with a good body of them in the head. The bristles should also have a fair degree of spring in them, especially where oil paints are being used.

For shellac polishes and spirit varnishes a softer bristle is to be preferred. Ideally, polisher's mops should be used. These are circular in shape with soft bristles or hairs, having a rounded or slightly pointed tip. They are available in different sizes, number 8 being a good general purpose size, well suited to home use.

Some workers prefer to fit a plywood 'hood' to the mop, holding it in place with a panel pin as shown in *Figure 7.1*. The

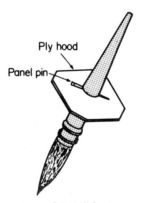

Figure 7.1. Polisher's mop

purpose of this is twofold: the hood acts as a cover for the jar in which the polish is contained, and it prevents the bristles from resting on the bottom of the container, where they would soon spread out and become useless. A paint brush distorted in such a manner is said to be 'crippled'. Signs of a good brush or mop are that the bristles hold together when wet, and keep a good shape.

Brushes need some care and attention if their maximum life potential is to be obtained. If they are going to be used again the following day they should be suspended overnight in a container of the appropriate thinners. After final use, wash out in clean thinners, dry out as much as possible with a clean rag then wash thoroughly with soap and hot water. Bristles should then be manipulated to a good shape and lightly tied with a rubber band before leaving to dry out.

The author prefers to wrap the head lightly with kitchen tissue as an aid to setting the shape while drying out, and wash out brushes after every session, in thinners. To get rid of excess thinners before re-using the brush, hold the handle between the palms of the hands and 'swizzle' the brush vigorously — taking care that the fine spray does not alight on anything vulnerable.

Rag is used during many of the finishing processes, apart from drying out brushes. This always should be clean, soft and most important, free from fluff. Sections of washed cotton garments are likely to be the best, but avoid wool.

Conditions for finishing

Physical conditions under which finishing is done are important. Good light is essential and where possible the arrangement should be to have adequate light on one side of the job being tackled, with the operative on the other, as in *Figure 7.2*. This is to allow the surface being treated to act as a reflector of the light from one side to the eyes of the person doing the finishing, on the other side. The reflection which the surface gives is a very important guide to the way the work is going.

The big enemy of most finishing processes is dust, particularly surfaces which remain tacky for several hours. Draughts must be avoided as far as possible as they create air currents by which particles of dust become mobile. Doors and windows should be kept closed as far as this is reasonably possible to minimise air movement.

Finishing is best carried out in a warm atmosphere of around 65° F, but avoid the use of fan heaters for obvious reasons. Most finishes dry better with gentle warmth, and the flow quality usually improves as the temperature is raised,

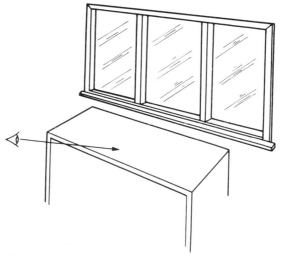

Figure 7.2. Position work near light source so that light is reflected on to the surface being tackled

within tolerable limits. Humidity is not good for finishing processes and the air should be reasonably dry. It is often convenient to carry out the finishing process in the after-noon or evening, when work with wet surfaces can be left to dry overnight in a closed room or workshop.

Finishing with oil paints

With an oil painted finish at least three coats are necessary. Before applying any paint, however, all knots or resin pockets should be coated with 'knotting'. Resin can exude through several coats of paint, and prevent some paints from drying properly. Knotting is a kind of thick, shellac varnish which dries quickly and seals in the resin. It should be feathered off at the edges so as not to cause ridges which will show under the paint.

Primers

The first coat of paint applied to new woodwork is referred to as the primer. Primers can be white, grey or pink in colour but their common quality is the ability to penetrate deeply into the wood fibres, adhere firmly and provide a solid base for subsequent rubbing down and following coats.

Aluminium primers for wood are becoming increasingly popular. It is claimed that they are more effective in sealing knots than the traditional material, and the author's experience confirms this. They should be well stirred before use, and frequently during use.

Standard primer can be thinned with white spirit to increase its penetrative powers in hard, dense wood or to seal off very absorbent surfaces. If this is done it may be necessary to apply another coat, to provide the body required for rubbing down. Primers, nonetheless, should be well brushed out and not applied thickly. If your primer does not brush out easily, thin it slightly with the recommended thinners.

Undercoats

The next coat is the undercoating, usually of a similar shade to the finishing one, but not invariably. This also provides body and a good, opaque base for the top coating. Two undercoats are even better but each one must be lightly rubbed down when dry.

Topcoats

The topcoat, gloss, satin or matt, provides protection to the undercoatings. It is a thin, tough but elastic film which will withstand dirt, many harmful vapours and the elements, and with some makes is slightly translucent to allow the colour of the undercoating to blend with it. Some paint makers advise two top coats for finest results. Satin is usually used indoors, matt invariably so.

A coat of oil paint should be left for at least 12 hours before follow-on treatment, although it may be touch dry before that time has elapsed. On the other hand, do not leave the following coat until the film has hardened. A dry surface and a hard one can be very different. Paint usually dries overnight but may take several days to harden. A fresh film will bond to the dry one but not so readily to it when it has hardened off.

Many modern paints are designed to short circuit the techniques described for oil paint with linseed or other vegetable oil as the vehicle and white spirit for the solvent. Oil paints are returning to favour because of the faults inherent with these modern paints. Craftsmen who make reproduction painted furniture would not use synthetic finishes.

Light rubbing down with fine abrasive should be carried out between one coat of paint and the next. This is known as 'flatting'. The purpose is to level the surface and free it from brush marks, runs and dust pimples, and provide a good 'key' for the next coat. Coarse paper will make scratches on the surface, which will show through the final coat, and may cut the ground back to bare wood. For very hard paint films and enamels wet-and-dry abrasive can be used, lubricated with water. Do not use this on bare wood. After flatting, the surface must be dry and well dusted before another coat is applied.

Paint should be applied relatively thinly. Never overload the brush as this results in runs and messy dripping. The brush is not used merely to apply the paint but to spread it out thoroughly and evenly. Brush tips are used with progressively lighter strokes as the paint is spread out from each brush-load. Only about two-thirds of the brush should be dipped in the paint and tips are then lightly wiped on the container edge to remove excess charge.

Each part of the surface should be brushed over several times, alternating across and with the grain. This is called 'crossing' and helps to ensure even coverage, and the avoidance of thick build-ups which can lead to runs and wrinkled drying.

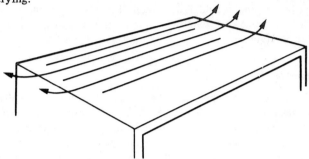

Figure 7.3. Work outwards with the brush, starting the stroke near to one end, and lift the brush off at the other

Figure 7.4. Dragging the brush inwards from the edge will result in runs

When a specific area has been evenly coated a final light brushing, along the grain and with only the brush tips, should be given. This is known as 'laying off' and the brush strokes should be parallel to one another, as in *Figure 7.3*.

Work away from the edge, starting some distance in from it, as arrowed in the drawing. Dragging the brush, fully charged, right from the edge will induce runs or 'tears' over the edge as in *Figure 7.4*. The brush should have lost most of its charge when it sweeps the opposite edge and the tip should be lifted so the bristles leave the work gently as it reaches the edge.

That may seem complicated but it really is quite easy. The manipulative skill with a brush is soon acquired. Just keep a flexible, sensitive touch, from the wrist and hold the brush lightly, as you would hold a pen. Do not apply the paint thickly — one-coat painting is for amateurs, and the results look amateurish.

Staining

Techniques when applying other finishes by brush are similar but results may be different. Most 'clear' finishes have a slight darkening effect on wood, usually similar to the change of colour seen when the wood is mopped with a wet cloth. Sometimes, however, the intention is to make the wood considerably darker than this but without reducing the grain and other patterns. A typical example is an item of reproduction furniture in oak. Time gives oak a beautiful mellow colour ranging from almost brown-black to a rich golden-brown. The rich red of old mahogany is also much simulated in reproduction work.

Producing colours or matching one colour to another is called 'staining'. A quite legitimate process in woodworking is staining strong but poorly coloured hardwoods to resemble better coloured but weaker — or more costly — species. Beech, for example, is often stained to resemble walnut or teak. We must add that the resemblance is only in colour — figure and grain will not be similar. Poorly coloured timber can, however be enriched to match perfect stock and the grain or figure will agree.

At one time stains would be made up by the polisher, as required. Invariably they would be made with powdered pigments obtainable from specialist shops, and mixed with water. Chemicals would also be used, mixed in water; in old books on finishing and in updated versions of old books these pigments and chemicals will still be quoted. They are not now so easy to find, although they are around, but excellent ready-mixed stains are available. Water stains penetrate well and are not 'fugitive' in the finishing material. Some, however, are earth pigments and produce a slight muddiness in the colour which gives the game away to an experienced eye. Pigments and dyes in alcohol are good and do not raise the grain like water stains, which is not much of a fault anyway, but the pigment may flow into the finish if it is also alcohol based, such as french polish. One other disadvantage is that the rapid evaporation of the alcohol makes it difficult to keep a wet edge going when staining large areas, with the result that streakiness and patches can occur easily.

Naptha stains are very common and extensively advertised these days. They penetrate well, do not dry too quickly and hold a wet edge, are intermixable and can be thinned quite readily with white spirit. They are excellent when used in conjunction with modern synthetic varnishes or oil varnishes but do not, in the author's experience, agree with shellac finishes or cellulose.

Thus staining is not just a matter of applying some colouring liquid to your woodwork. The stain must be compatible with the finishing material, and water soluble stains appear to be the nearest to a universal stain that we can find.

When you have the stain, try it out first on a piece of scrap wood of the same type as the workpiece, or in an unseen corner. If necessary, dilute the stain so that it is a little lighter than required — you can always apply some more. When the stain dries give it a coat or generous rub of the finish. Establish that you have the colour required, bearing in mind that it is easy to tone down too light a colour but almost impossible to reduce one that is too dark.

Whatever stain is used the method of application is basically the same. It can be applied by brush or pad of cotton wool wrapped in a cloth, which is easier and gives a more uniform coverage. on large areas. Work with the grain and apply fairly liberally so that streakiness is avoided, but bearing in mind the nature of the surface being copied, matched or 'created'. When applying stain, or a clear finish, always keep the wet edge parallel to the grain, which is also the direction of application, as in *Figure 7.5 (b)*. If applied across the grain as in (*a*), marks could be left on the surface.

End grain must be treated with care. It is very absorbent and will come up much darker than faces of the timber if the same quantity of stain is used. It may be a good plan to seal

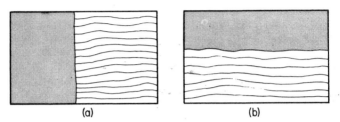

Figure 7.5. Do not apply stain or clear finish across the grain as at (a), but keep the wet edge parallel to the grain as at (b), to avoid leaving marks on the surface

end grain before staining, with some well diluted finishing material. Then use diluted stain in one or more coats, as required.

Surfaces, also, may be patchy with areas of 'woolly', interlocked, reversed or soft grain. Areas such as these may take up more stain than the rest, or it may go in more deeply, causing dark patches. Filling may have reduced the risk but a weak sealer coat may be advisable if a stroke with a water-charged brush indicates extra absorbency areas.

If darker streaks have to be introduced deliberately in order to match, use artists' or pencil brushes, after the base coat of stain is dry. When all staining is completed the work must be well rubbed down with the finest grade abrasive, following the grain, and then dusted off until quite clean. Vacuum dusting is best if finishing is to follow in the same room because dust can float around for hours after brushing off.

Staining does no more than change the colour of wood. It is not in itself a finish although there is a range of varnish stains which provides a dual role. There is a proper sequence of applying the stain to a construction: an example of the correct sequence of applying stain (and any type of general

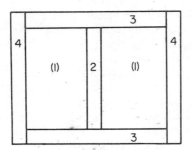

Figure 7.6. Sequence for applying stain to a framed assembly (see text)

finish) is shown in *Figure 7.6*. First treat the panels (1), then muntins (2), rails (3) and stiles (4). This sequence avoids the bad practice of cross-grain brushing where joints occur.

Varnishes

At one time varnishes were considered to have relatively poor drying qualities, especially in colder than normal temperatures. They did not like humid conditions and proof of this would be displayed by a grape-like bloom on a varnished surface affected by damp air. Copal, carriage and similar varnishes are still used for high-class work when appearance, durability and weather resistance are the first requirements.

Modern synthetic varnishes are much quicker drying than the oil types but can also be temperamental. Polyurethane varnishes are tough, resist abrasion reasonably, are easy to apply when atmospheric conditions are favourable (not cold or humid) but appear to lack the penetrative power and adhesion, and the solar ray resistance of older types of varnish. This is, of course, a generalisation and these finishes are still being improved upon and fortified in the light of experience and research by the chemists who created them.

The polyurethanes generally have a good flow and do not need extensive brushing out. They can withstand temperatures up to that of boiling water, many acids and alcohol mixtures.

At least two coats of varnish are needed and up to four, depending on the nature of the wood and the particular type of finish required. As with paint, the first coat should be diluted for extra penetration, but always follow the maker's instructions in this respect. All coats except the final one should be lightly rubbed down and dusted before the next. Some woods, particularly the softer ones, are more absorbent than others and in consequence require an extra coat.

Modern varnishes are available in three distinct types, drying out according to the particular texture required for the finished surface. They are gloss, eggshell (or satin) and matt finish. The first provides a high gloss, accentuated by the quality of preparation, and easy to clean surface. The eggshell finish leaves a pleasing satiny sheen which is nowadays very popular and the third provides a well-bodied surface without gloss or sheen. It is not suitable for outdoor use or in situations where a lot of dirt is produced, as this clings to the matt surface and can be difficult to remove.

When an eggshell or matt finish is required the undercoating should be glossy; with a gloss finish the opposite is the case. Do not apply a finishing coat directly to the wood surface – it will simply sink in, unevenly, and provide a blotchy base for following coats.

Some modern finishes, however, can be applied coat-on-coat and are claimed to provide a one-coat finish. But, they have limitations not immediately apparent yet obvious to anyone who can appreciate a first-class job.

Some manufacturers offer a range of 'coloured' varnishes. The colours are of two broad varieties, one being the shades of traditionally treated furniture woods: dark oak, rich mahogany, teak, and so on. The idea is to combine the purpose of a stain with a varnish and thus colour pale or cheaper wood to imitate the more expensive kind. Such varnishes have their place and are useful, in particular when on restoration work of a domestic nature. They must be applied carefully from the point of the brush to obtain an even flow, as uneven coating will result in patchiness. Each coat applied will make the surface darker so, when the required colour is obtained and a further coat is needed to build up body or gloss, a compatible clear varnish (by the same maker, if possible) should be used.

The other type of coloured varnish is pigmented by the addition of bright dyes in basic colours: orange, green, yellow and many others. They act rather like translucent paint, giving a bold colour to the work but allowing the grain to show through. They are useful on kitchen projects and for nursery furniture or toys.

Spirit varnish offers a quick-drying alternative to oil varnish and is particularly suitable for small jobs. It is made from shellac with the addition of a gum such as sandarac, dissolved in industrial alcohol. Methylated spirit is a thinner or solvent. Because alcohol evaporates rapidly, especially in a warm atmosphere, spirit varnish dries quickly. As a result, several coats can be applied in the time it would take one coat of oil varnish to dry and the freshly applied surface remains tacky for a short while only. It is therefore less likely to be affected by dust in the atmosphere.

The varnish must be applied evenly and quickly, with particular attention to brushing out as it does not flow out so readily as oil varnish. Rubbing down between coats is essential or the final surface will be very uneven.

Polishes

French polish is also shellac and alcohol formulated. Traditional french polishing requires a fair degree of skill on the operative's part and the technique of this process is outside the scope of this book. French polishing can, however, be done in a simplified way, with satisfactory results for the amount of time and skill involved.

Between three and six coats of polish should be applied, thinly and evenly – preferably using a polishers' mop. Rubbing down between coats is an essential part of this process but, as the film of polish is very thin, flatting must be done with the finest grade of abrasive paper: 00 or 'flour'. If a high shine is required the last coat can be left as applied by the mop.

Alternatively the final coat can be flatted like the others and then waxed. A good quality furniture wax will do, applied rather thinly and well rubbed in. The surface is finally burnished with a clean, soft duster.

Some workers prefer to apply the wax with very fine steel wool, which further abrades the shellac and therefore continues to level out the surface. Whatever method is used the final result is a semi-gloss type of finish which is quite popular and pleasant to handle. The waxing can periodically be repeated if the surface needs a tonic and restoration of lustre.

The techniques can be modified slightly to leave a matt finish. Coating is continued, as before, to build up what is called a 'body' and the final, dry coat is rubbed down with fine steel wool, used dry. Rubbing must be with the grain or very fine scratches made by the wool will be visible.

Most shellac polishes and varnishes are orange-brown in colour, depending on the particular type of shellac used. This includes orange, button and garnet. They all have a slight darkening effect on the wood but if the wood is very dark in colour this is insignificant. Problems arise with light coloured or mixed woods, where the work would be spoilt using a polish of this type — as, for example, in inlaying or marquetry work. For any job where the colour of the wood is to be retained as natural as possible, white french polish should be used. White polish is made from orange shellac which has been bleached.

Shellac finishes are only suitable for indoor use as they rapidly break down if exposed to the elements. They also mark very easily, particularly from heat and water, and spillage from alcoholic drinks can ruin the surface.

Wax polishing is a fairly simple process and is one of the oldest methods of finishing woodwork. It is considered especially suitable for oak, leaving as it does a surface with a very mellow 'feel'. Because waxing has only limited qualities of adequately filling the grain, there is a danger that a wholly waxed finish will, after a period of time, tend to pick up a certain amount of dirt. Waxing is therefore not particularly suitable for light coloured woods, and when used now with oak this is usually when the wood has been stained, often quite dark, to simulate an antique finish.

In order to seal off any staining from the effects wax may have and also to act as a foundation and help keep out the dirt, it is common practice with this form of finish to give one or two coats of french polish over the stain, before waxing.

An effective way of applying wax polish is by using a small brush, such as a shoe brush. The wax should be brushed on thoroughly and liberally then left for several hours to harden off. Next, as with shoe polishing, another brush is used to bring up the shine and a soft duster for final burnishing.

Wax polish can quite easily be made at home. The principal ingredients are pure beeswax, a little carnauba wax, and pure terpentine. The wax is shredded into a shallow tin, covered with turpentine and left until the wax disolves. Final consistency should be like soft butter. Slight variations of the above recipe exclude the carnauba wax, which is exceedingly hard, or involve addition of other substances and heating to speed up the process. Turpentine, however, has a low flash point and great care is needed.

Waxing is the sort of finish which improves with the passage of time, providing periodic re-waxing and the all-important burnishing operations are carried out.

Oiling

Oiling the wood as a means of finishing has seen a revival of popularity in recent years. This is probably because of the preference for a natural finish with minimal shine, which is the effect given by oils. It is also quite suitable for teak – an oily wood – and veneered chipboard constructions with their large plain surfaces.

Traditionally linseed oil, which slowly oxidises when exposed to the air, was used but it is slow to dry and picks up dirt easily. Modern oil preparations are usually sold under the name of 'teak oil', but they can be used on almost any timber.

Application is simple: the oil is wiped on generously with a cloth, rubbed well in and the surplus then mopped off. After leaving for several hours a second application is given. Oiling has only very slight grain filling qualities and is more suited to darker coloured woods because of dirt-retaining properties. As with waxing, it can be re-done at intervals and the body of the finish builds up in a similar manner.

Lacquers

Plastic lacquers offer a modern way of finishing home-built furniture projects. Most set by a chemical reaction brought about by the addition of a catalyst or hardener. Only enough for the job in hand is prepared because once the catalyst is added the action is irreversible. Coatings can be generous and they flow out evenly. Setting is entirely by chemical action, not evaporation or oxidisation, so the process is quite rapid. Thorough flatting between coats will result in a beautiful surface finish, and wet-or-dry papers are required for best results, using water or white spirit as a lubricant. Flatted surfaces must, of course, be well cleaned off and quite dry before following coatings are applied. Use grade 400 or 500 to avoid scratching and continue until all traces of shine are removed from the surface, which must be free from ridges or hollows.

The final lustre is obtained by use of a burnishing cream and the shine will be in proportion to the amount of rubbing which the surface receives. A power drill fitted with a polishing bonnet can speed up the burnishing work considerably. As these lacquers are so hard a very high shine can be produced by burnishing. This is known as a 'mirror-finish'. It can also be waxed to a satin sheen or left matt, as in the waxing process previously described.

Because this type of lacquer requires a fairly thick film, built up from relatively liberal coatings, the polish is at its best when applied to flat, horizontal surfaces. It is therefore ideal for table tops, especially as it is highly resistant to scratching and marking from heat and liquids. Some, in fact, will resist the heat of a smouldering cigarette.

Emulsion paints

For certain kinds of toys and nursery projects, decorators'
emulsion paints offer a cheap and simple way of providing a
finish. White emulsion can also be used as a primer/sealer for
hardboard which has to be painted. Emulsions have the
advantage of being quick drying and they have good covering
properties. For most jobs two coats are sufficient, but to protect
the surface from finger marks one or two coats of clear varnish
can subsequently be applied.

Creosote

Sometimes wood is given a finishing treatment more to protect
it from decay than anything else. By far the most common
treatment is creosote. It is still a popular way of protecting
garden fencing, sheds, greenhouses and similar outbuildings.

At its simplest creosote is just brushed on, the more coats
the better. The treatment is renewed every two or three
years. For fencing posts and any timber in contact with the
ground a better process is to immerse the lower part in a
container of creosote for several days, or even weeks. Timber
should be well seasoned as the drier it is the more it will
absorb the fluid. Creosote has also a decorative effect as it
stains the wood brown. It is available in light or dark shades.
Once wood has been treated with creosote it cannot be
painted as the 'tar' will eventually bleed through the paint,
even though it appears to be dry and fit for painting.

Where it is desired to give a painted finish combined with
a decay inhibitor, then one of the proprietory solutions, such
as Cuprinol clear should be used. It is applied in the same way
as creosote.

So much for finishing. We have only touched the fringe of
the subject but hope the object of this Chapter has been
achieved. Your woodworking project, whether it be a fencing
post or a reproduction piece of furniture, will ultimately be
only as good as the finish applied.

8 Basic Constructions

Historical background

Wood is one of man's most widely used raw materials. Such is the great variety of purposes for which wood can be used that, over a long period of time, many quite separate crafts evolved. These divisions of woodworking developed largely according to the nature of the end product. Because of new materials, new ideas, new technologies and changes in social life or customs some of these crafts, which were still thriving at the beginning of the century, have all but passed into history. Carriage and cart building, wheel-making and coopering (making barrels) are three where great difficulty would be experienced in finding a practising craftsman. Yet more wood is now being used than ever before, and through good 'harvesting', re-planting and conservation the supply will continue to meet demand.

Revival of interest has in some cases led to a resurgence of craftsmanship in many areas of woodworking. Marquetry, carving, musical instruments, toy-making, turnery and boat-building again are thriving activities. Indeed, in small boat-building the pendulum of favour has now swung back towards using wood for this most traditional of crafts.

Principal crafts

Despite the many branches of woodworking, the three major ones have always been, and still are, carpentry, joinery and furniture-making. It is true that the nature of the work done under these headings changes as time goes by. For instance, the amount of solid wood used in furniture making has decreased while the amount of chipboard continues to be on the increase. This means a change, or for many an extension, in the skills needed for the craft as the techniques required for the wise use of a different material are learned and mastered.

Carpentry

Carpentry is often thought of as rough work, with only limited skills. This may be true of some individuals but is more likely not to be so. Carpentry does frequently involve using wood 'in the rough' meaning timber straight from the saw and in situations where to plane it would be a waste of time and money. This branch of woodworking tends to use

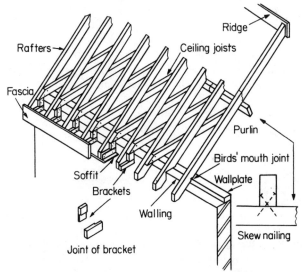

Figure 8.1. Typical carpentry work − roof construction

a large volume of wood in relation to the amount of labour put into it, and building operations still include a lot of carpentry, as in roofing, illustrated in *Figure 8.1*.

Floors and roofs are two of the main parts of a building where the work is classed as carpentry. Even on a building where floors and roofs are no longer of timber it is still very probable that the carpenter has played a significant part.

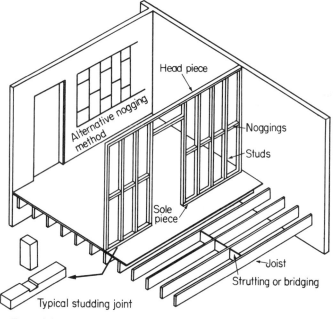

Figure 8.2. Typical carpentry work – construction of floor and partition

Floors of concrete, and roofs and stairs of the same material, need temporary moulds or supports for the concrete in its wet state. Wood is used far more than any other material for this purpose and this is an area of carpentry which has been growing in recent years. This temporary supporting of concrete work is known as shuttering or formwork; it has indeed almost become a sub-branch of carpentry.

In building work, many interior walls which are non-load-bearing are often referred to as partition walls. Frequently these are made of timber in the form of a framing, known as 'studded partitions'. The stud is the vertical member of this framework. *Figure 8.2* shows a typical example, with the various parts named. Vertical timbers are positioned at 406 mm (16 in) centres, as are floor and ceiling joists, because the usual method of cladding such a partition is by plaster board which is nailed to the studding and then 'skimmed' with plaster. Plaster board, and other sheet materials such as plywood, hardwood, wall and insulation board, all have a standard width of 1220 mm (48 in). Joints, therefore, coincide with centres of the supporting timbers without cutting and waste.

Figures 8.1 and *8.2* illustrate typical carpentry work examples (by no means complete) of a building nature, along with the usual names for components involved. Joints in common use for this work are also shown. Trenches, both through and stopped, are frequently used, as are half-laps of one type or another. A simple joint much used on roofing work of traditional nature is a notch cut on an angle to suit the slope of the roof. It is employed where a rafter crosses the wall plate and is called a bird's mouth. Many of the members are nailed together from the side. This is called 'skew nailing', and is illustrated in *Figure 8.1*.

Joinery

Joinery work includes making and fitting doors, windows, staircases and the fitting out of a building to its purpose, e.g. the fitting of counters in a bank and shelves in a library.

Joiners nearly always work with 'prepared' timber, also known as planed, dressed or wrot. Joinery is invariably visible and therefore would go through a finishing process. The most common finish for joinery is paint, although hardwood joinery (another sub-division of the trade) is more often varnished or polished.

Sometimes a craftsman may be described as a carpenter and joiner. This is common in building work where the joinery is usually of softwood. The most common softwood used is red deal, also called redwood. It is sometimes referred to by its country of origin, hence names like Baltic red, Scandinavian or Russian redwood. As with all timbers the quality varies but the best is selected for joinery and is often called joinery quality or joinery redwood.

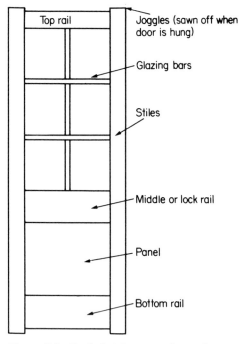

Figure 8.3. Typical joinery work – door construction

Other softwoods used by the joiner include whitewood, hemlock and Columbian pine. The joiner may find himself using the same range of hardwoods used by the furniture industry, and here the range is very wide. Teak, iroko, mahogany, walnut and oak are some of the long established hardwoods to be seen alongside those of more recent introduction.

The door shown in *Figure 8.3* is a typical piece of joinery of the frame type. (We will explain what we mean by 'frame' later on.) In a better class product the joints would be through mortise and tenons. Many doors, however, are imported and these frequently are of dowelled construction. This method, properly applied with sound materials and adhesives, is quite satisfactory for domestic-class doors.

Joggles, or horns, are left on for two reasons. The first is that it is wise to leave on some waste when a mortise is

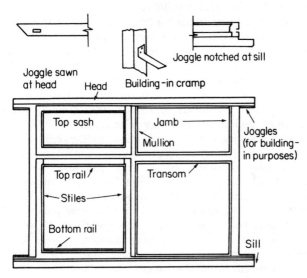

Figure 8.4. Typical joinery work — window construction

being cut near the end. This reduces the risk of the wood splitting at this point, especially if the joint is secured by wedging. The second reason, which applies to all doors whatever the pattern or mode of construction, is that the joggle projecting at a corner protects the door from damage during storage and transporting and before being hung.

Windows are made in almost every conceivable size and pattern, in both softwood and hardwood. Although many windows are mass produced to comply with British Standards specifications governing window sizes, materials and construction, a high proportion of windows outside the area of housing are 'specials' of one sort or another. Most, however, have certain features in common and *Figure 8.4* shows a typical window and the names of the various parts. This is also an example of framed construction.

Fairly large joggles are left on the head and sill of a window frame. They are used for 'building-in' purposes but they also protect the joinery during handling and transportation.

The usual practice on domestic type buildings is for the windows to be positioned into the brickwork as the wall is built. The sill joggles are usually notched to fit around the wall while the head joggles are sawn on the splay so as to allow the projecting part to be built in the wall. Exterior door frames have similar joggles and, while building practices regarding building-in sills vary a little, sides of frames are fixed in masonry joints by hoop-iron or similar cramps screwed to the frames. These features are illustrated in *Figure 8.4*.

An item of joinery that has been around for very many years is the door shown in *Figure 8.5*. This is known as the ledged and braced door. Smaller and cheaper ones are made without the diagonal braces and are called braced doors. While the braces add a great deal to the rigidity of the door this also means that the door becomes 'handed' because, in order to gain full benefit from the braces, these members must slope upwards from the hanging side. This door is also an example of a construction which does not fit into any of the three main types of classification discussed later, although it can be thought of as a fore-runner to the frame.

Ledged and braced doors are a good example of construction which relies almost entirely on nailing. Usually, oval nails are chosen which will penetrate the battens by about 13 mm ($\frac{1}{2}$ in). The nails are driven in from the front and punched well home then the projecting points are hammered flat on the battens. Punching down on the end of the nails ensure that they are

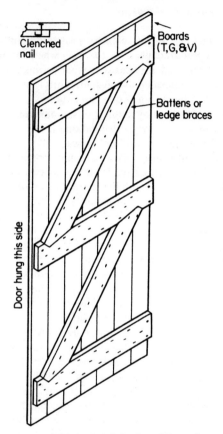

*Figure 8.5. Typical ledged and braced
door*

slightly below the surface. This method of nailing is known as
'clenching', and is illustrated in *Figure 8.5*. For extra strength
ends of the ledges are often secured by a couple of screws. The
braces can have a simple notching arrangement as shown, or
merely be butted against the ledges.

Furniture and cabinet making

Furniture making in this country has its origins going back four or five hundred years to the days when the majority of the population lived in villages or small towns and when one of the principal craftsmen of the community was the carpenter. Chests, settles, tables and sideboard-cupboards were the main items made. Mortise and tenon joints abounded and the most common timber was oak. Decoration, if any, was by relief carving and the finish was oil or beeswax.

Eventually furniture making became a separate craft and English furniture reached its zenith about two hundred years ago in the days of elegant living for the privileged few and miserable poverty for the vast majority.

Most people connected with the furniture industry agree that furniture making went through a bad time in the years between the two world wars. Possibly it was a reflection of the times but the standards of construction, workmanship and finish were regarded as poor. Naturally there were exceptions but the bulk of mass-produced suites during this time were in most cases made with complete regard to a single over-riding factor: price. Quality had to suffer.

Most manufacturers of any note now employ trained designers. This fact alone has elevated the standard of much of what we see offered for sale. New materials introduced a few years ago are now well proven, and this is particularly true of man-made boards. Chipboard has possibly been the biggest single influence on the trends in cabinet making, along with melamine plastics surfaces and laminated sheet, or in the form of other synthetic surfaces coated on to a board during manufacture.

Basic forms of construction

Woodworking constructions are generally of three basic types: frame, stool and box. Many are a combination of two forms while others involve all three. Some projects, however, cannot be conveniently classified into any particular type.

The chest is one of the earliest pieces of furniture and in the primitive form was of box construction. This would be made from wide boards, or a series of boards side by side. The earliest jointing would have been by crude nails or wooden pegs. Shrinkage of wood, more pronounced in wide boards, always creates problems. Whichever way the direction of grain was combined there was always a conflict of side grain with lengthways grain. As wood shrinks across the grain, but not

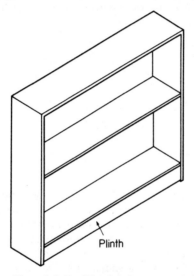

Plinth

Figure 8.6. Small bookshelves – a typical box construction

lengthways, splits and distortion took place. Over the years techniques have been evolved which make allowance for the fact that solid boards, especially wide ones, are likely to shrink and sometimes swell.

Broadly, shrinkage takes place during seasoning but wood can re-absorb moisture under damp conditions and as a result swell then subsequently shrink again when conditions become drier. This is a very significant factor which has influenced construction methods over the last few years in many specific ways, as we shall explain.

Returning to box constructions, they are to be found a great deal in cabinet making. *Figure 8.6* shows a simple example of a set of open bookshelves. Although these days material forming the bookshelves may be of veneered chipboard, the use of other man-made boards does not alter the overall style, only the details such as jointing and methods of adding the back. In this example the plinth is shown as an integral part of the assembly.

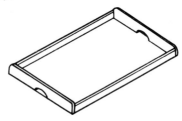

Figure 8.7. Simple tea tray is essentially a shallow box

A simple tea tray is shown in *Figure 8.7*. While hardly an example of cabinet making as such it is another example of box construction. It has four sides and a bottom, and although the sides are narrow it can more conveniently be thought of as a box rather than a frame.

Figure 8.8 illustrates a simple stool, although it is not of stool construction. It is of box form, even though there are only three sides to the box; rails are introduced as alternatives to the sides.

Most stools and tables are based on stool construction. Broadly, stool construction can be thought of as a three-dimensional framework where the members are relatively narrow compared with the overall size involved.

A basic form of stool construction is shown in *Figure 8.9*, where the same arrangement of legs and rails could be used for a dining table, small occasional table or stool. The cross-sectional sizes of the legs and rails, their positioning in relation

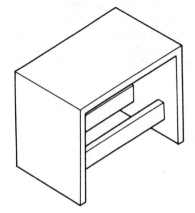

Figure 8.8. Stool of box construction

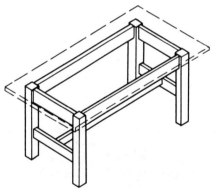

*Figure 8.9. Most stools and tables are
examples of stool construction*

to one another and the range of joints and variations to these
joints are almost without limit. These factors, along with others
such as proportion and shaping, form the basis of designing,
and explain why even for a project like an occasional table the
number of designs which can be produced is very large.

For stools, a fairly common variation to the use of legs which are rectangular in cross section is to use dowelling, as shown in *Figure 8.10.* When cabinet- and chair-making were in their heyday many parts of a piece of furniture were produced by the woodturner on his lathe. Chair legs were often turned

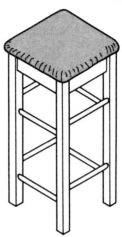

Figure 8.10. Kitchen stool in which all the lower rails are dowels

for at least part of their length and rails frequently for the whole length, when they were sometimes known as spindles. Using a dowel for a rail is a simplified version of a spindle where, in both cases, the rail is joined to the leg by a hole being bored in the leg to correspond with the diameter at the end of the rail. For both functional and appearance reasons it is possible to use metal tubing such as polished aluminium alloy for the lower rails, which also serve as footrests.

The sideboard illustrated in *Figure 8.11* shows a combination of constructional styles. The main part of the sideboard is known as the carcase, and this is of box construction. The same applies to the drawers. The underframing is made up as a separate part and is of stool construction.

Figure 8.12 shows the early chest referred to previously, while *Figure 8.13* illustrates a panelled version, evolved and constructed to overcome the difficulties of using wide boards and the problems associated with this mode of construction.

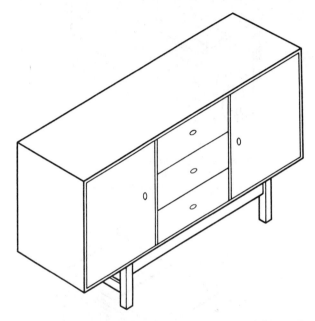

Figure 8.11. Sideboard shows a combination of box and stool constructions

Before the introduction of plywood and other man-made boards the panels were, of course, made from solid wood, but the construction allowed the panels to shrink or swell without this affecting the job overall, and eliminated the likelihood of splitting taking place. Although the chest is in the form of a box the construction shown in *Figure 8.13* is a combination of stool for the body of the chest and flat frame for the lid.

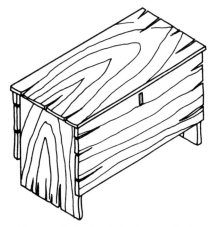

Figure 8.12. Early plank chest – splitting was inevitable because of wide boards and combination of grain direction

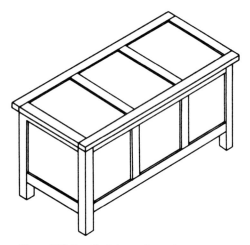

Figure 8.13. Panelled chest – framed construction allows for shrinkage of panels

Shrinkage and swelling

The problems associated with the shrinkage of timber during seasoning or drying out were known to early craftsmen but it took time for these difficulties to be overcome. Timber is to some extent hygroscopic. This means it acts in the same way as a sponge and releases moisture to the air during favourable atmospheric conditions, re-absorbing it during very humid

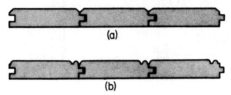

(a)

(b)

Figure 8.14. Sections through a ledged and braced door: (a) tongue and groove with Vee, (b) tongue and groove with bead

conditions. When this happens the wood shrinks or swells accordingly. This is the reason why external doors often stick in the winter time but operate quite satisfactorily during the warmer and normally drier months of the year.

Figure 8.14 shows a cross section through the boards of a ledged and braced door (*Figure 8.5*). Such doors should be assembled with the boards only loosely fitting; if dry boards are assembled and cramped up under dry conditions, subsequent swelling is almost bound to take place if the doors are used externally, as they usually are, and this would lead to distortion. The tongues and grooves are to hold the boards in alignment, and also to prevent gaps from appearing under conditions of shrinkage. The V and bead moulding is partly decorative and partly to conceal what otherwise might become a very obvious gap.

Weather boarding is often used as a cladding material on sheds and garages, and even houses. *Figure 8.15* shows two popular types. Not only is the method of rebating one piece to the other a form of jointing, it is also the device by which shrinkage is catered for without the weather-shielding characteristics being diminished.

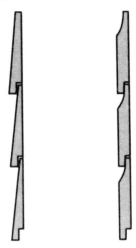

Figure 8.15. Types of vertical weather boarding in section

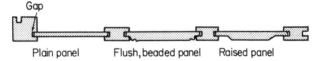

Figure 8.16. Types of solid panel in section, showing gaps

The principle behind panelled construction is to provide a framework of members which are grooved along their edges. Panels are fitted into these grooves. A panel must not be so tight that it cannot move, and there should be a slight gap between the panel and the bottom of the groove. *Figure 8.16* shows such a panel, along with variations in panelling design.

Ideally, the best kind of solid wood for panels is known as radial sawn. Cross shrinkage is at its least on boards sawn this way and the panels are likely to remain flat. (That is also why musical instrument soundboards are made from radial sawn timber.) Hardwoods, especially oak, have the most attractive grain and figure patterns when radial sawn.

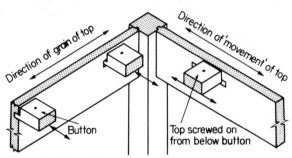

Figure 8.17. Use of buttons for securing a solid top to a table

The use of 'buttons' for securing a solid top to a table is now a very old established way of holding what can be a quite large area of wood (*Figure 8.17*). At the same time they allow the all-important freedom for the top to move, which in a large table could be quite considerable. The small mortises into which the buttons engage are made rather wider than the buttons; this applies especially to the rail which will be at right angles to the grain of the top. Mortises should also be made so that when the button is inserted it is not quite level with the upper edge of the rail. This is to ensure that the screw used to secure the top will hold it tight against the rail. When screwing the top in place the buttons on the rails which are parallel to the grain of the top should not be fully inserted into the mortises, again to allow for free movement.

As a modern alternative to buttons, shrinkage plates can be used. Two patterns are shown in *Figure 8.18*. For one, it is necessary to cut a recess in the rail, as shown. The angled type can also be used for other assembly work, such as fixing a plinth to the main carcase.

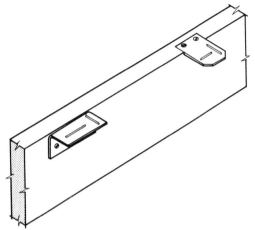

Figure 8.18. Shrinkage plates may be used as an alternative to buttons

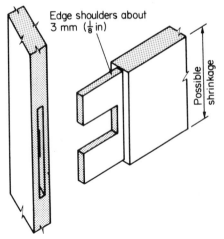

Figure 8.19. Edge shoulders are used on wide rails, to prevent formation of a gap due to shrinkage

Where a fairly wide rail is being tenoned into a stile the tenon is often cut with small edge shoulders. The purpose of this is twofold: a wide rail, as shown in *Figure 8.19,* can shrink slightly and if tenons were cut to the edge of the rail a small gap would result. Many craftsmen, however, feel it is good

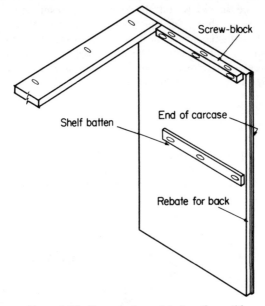

Figure 8.20. Slot-screwing minimises the problem
of wood shrinkage across the grain

practice to cut small edge shoulders wherever this is reasonably practicable, as it always conceals the end of the mortise and makes for a better job.

Edge shoulders are always formed on good quality cabinet work but rarely on softwood joinery. One reason for this is that in joinery the edges of a rail, as shown, would in all probability be either rebated for glass or grooved for a panel. Both of these cuts mean that the edge of the joint becomes hidden anyway. This would be exactly the case in the middle rail of the door shown in *Figure 8.3*, the lower edge being grooved and the upper one rebated.

It is often required to fix a batten across the grain of part of a carcase. Such a situation is shown in *Figure 8.20*. Here again there is a conflict of grain direction, where solid fixing by glue and screws would almost certainly result in trouble. By making the holes for the screws in the form of slots, the solid side with the screws in it is free to move. This technique is known as slot-screwing. The piece supporting the shelf is usually referred to as a batten, while the upper one, fixed to the top, is called a screw-block.

Framing joints

Simple types of framework members can be joined in a number of ways, *Figure 8.21* showing a typical selection. Half-lap joints can be employed in a number of different forms.

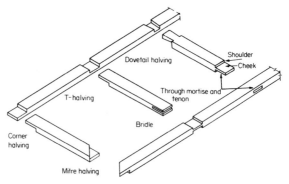

Figure 8.21. A selection of joints for framework members

Corner-halving for the corners and T-halving for the intermediate members are the most straightforward. As the name suggests, half the wood is removed on each part of the joint. Where one side of the frame will be visible, the mitre halving has a neater appearance; where there might be a tendency for the frame to be pulled apart the dovetail version has certain self-locking characteristics.

The dovetailed halving is probably the most basic form of dovetail joint. *Figure 8.22* shows the limits of the slope used in all dovetail joints, a slope of 1 in 6 being considered more suitable for softwoods while a slope of 1 in 8 is generally regarded as being more suited to hardwoods. Some craftsmen settle for a 1 in 7 slope for all timbers.

Also shown in *Figure 8.21* is the mortise and tenon joint in its most elementary form, and a bridle joint. In practice, the

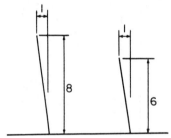

Figure 8.22. Limits of slope for dovetail joints

bridle would not be used in the type of framing shown as it would leave a very thin 'neck' in the rail. The bridle is, however, a useful joint with other applications to be discussed later.

The mortise and tenon joint is the most widely used joint in woodwork. It has been estimated that the number of variations of this joint run into thousands but some basic forms are shown in *Figure 8.23*.

For a joint which is at the corner of a framework such as a door the haunched joint (*a*) is usual. The haunch (H) is made about one-third the width of the wood (W), while the thickness of the tenon is one-third, or slightly more, the thickness of the wood. The haunched mortise and tenon has itself a number of varieties. It can be 'through' or 'stopped', with or without a rebate, with or without a groove, and so on. An ordinary through joint is shown at (*b*).

A blind mortise and stub tenon joint (*c*) are really the same type of joint. It is also known as a stopped mortise and tenon. The proportional length of the tenon can vary. For location purposes only, the tenon can be quite short, but for maximum

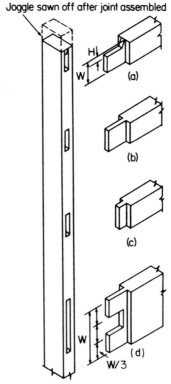

Joggle sawn off after joint assembled

Figure 8.23. Some basic forms of mortise and tenon joint

strength the mortise should be cut as deeply as possible without penetrating the member and the tenon made fractionally shorter than this depth. For all blind mortise and tenon joints there should be a slight gap at the end of the tenon in order to ensure tightness at the shoulder.

Hard and fast rules cannot be laid down to decide at what point the tenon in a wide rail should be made into double tenons (*d*). The governing factor is the mortise: too long a mortise in a thin member will weaken it, particularly if it is a through joint. Where the width of the wood (W) exceeds about 4 times its thickness, double tenons are used with a centre haunch. The length of a haunch from the shoulders equals the thickness of the tenon. The purpose behind a double tenon is to make the tenon in two parts with solid

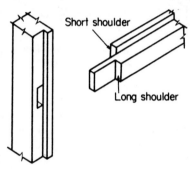

Figure 8.24. Long and short shoulders,
for rebated members

wood left between them so that strength is not impaired. The tenon is continuous haunched for a shallow depth in order to keep the member 'in-line' and provide a clean, tight joint in the finished work.

It is frequently required to rebate the edge of material which is to be mortised and tenoned. The rebate must be allowed for in both parts of the joint. *Figure 8.24* provides an example. Shoulders of the tenon are not level, the one on the rebated side must be made nearer to the end by an amount equal to the depth of the rebate. The rebate will also cut away part of the tenon, so reducing its width. The extent of the mortise must, therefore, be diminished accordingly. This tenon is said to have 'long and short shoulders'.

A rebate does not necessarily line up with the edge of the tenon as in *Figure 8.24,* but may come part way across the tenon as in *Figure 8.25 (a).* In this case the tenon must be further cut to the form shown at (*b*) and the mortise made to suit this.

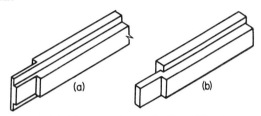

Figure 8.25. Where a rebate coincides with a tenon, as at (a), the tenon must be further cut as at (b)

For a panelled frame edges of the material have to be grooved as a means of holding the panels. Here again the joint will be affected. Because it is very much easier to form grooves from end to end wherever this is feasible, the mortise and tenon have to be adjusted to suit. *Figure 8.26 (a)* illustrates this type of joint as required for a corner. The groove on the rail cuts away part of the tenon, so the mortise is made narrower by an amount equal to the depth of the groove. Because the mortised member is grooved right through, the tenon has to be prepared with a square haunch. This serves to fill what would otherwise be a gap. For a wide rail in such a frame, as often occurs at the bottom, double tenons may be desirable as shown in *Figure 8.26 (b).* If so, the tenons and the spaces are made approximately one fourth of the width available. If the groove is narrower than the joint, adjustments have to be made in a similar way as for rebated material.

It is generally considered easier and more straightforward in work of this kind to cut the joints first, then make the grooves or rebates. Rebates in doors and frames are the usual way of supporting and holding glass, bedded in putty and retained by glass sprigs and putty or wooden beads which may be pinned or screwed to the frame.

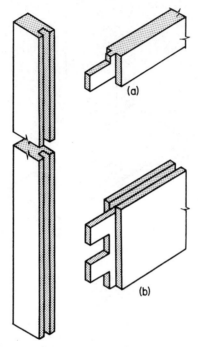

Figure 8.26. (a) Joint for corner of grooved frame, with square haunch to fill groove, (b) double tenons formed in wide rail, with haunch in centre and at edge

Sometimes it is necessary to form a mortise and tenon joint on the face of the wood, rather than on the edge. *Figure 8.27* shows this sort of situation. This type of joint is known as twin tenons. Note that the twin tenons are side by side, as distinct from the in-line double tenons.

Where a thinner member is being jointed to a wider one, as in *Figure 8.28,* it is wise to increase the thickness of the tenon above the usual one-third rule. This provides for a stronger

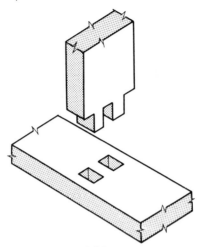

Figure 8.27. Twin tenons

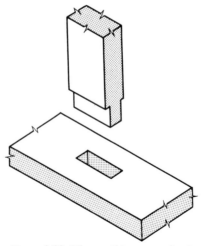

Figure 8.28. Where a thinner member is being jointed to a wider one, the thickness of the tenon may be increased

tenon, and therefore a stronger joint. Thus the shoulders are kept quite small to provide a tenon around half the thickness of the member. If the piece being tenoned is very thin, as in

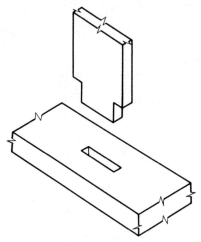

Figure 8.29. Where a very thin piece is being tenoned, edge shoulders only are made

Figure 8.29, it might be impracticable to form shoulders in the normal way, so edge shoulders only should be made, as illustrated.

Stool and box joints

The corner of a table, as shown in *Figure 8.30,* illustrates the application of the type of tenon called 'bare faced'. This has a shoulder on one side only. If the tenon were to be positioned in the centre of the rail it would mean that the mortise in the leg would be very near the edge of the wood, thus creating a weak spot. Where two tenons meet at right angles, as they do in a leg of the type illustrated, the usual way of obtaining maximum length for both tenons is to mitre the ends but always so as to leave a small gap between the mitred edges. In the example shown a small edge shoulder is included in the

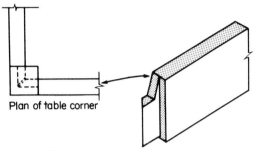

Plan of table corner

Figure 8.30. Bare-faced tenon, with sloping haunch and mitred end, suitable for a table corner

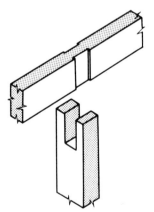

Figure 8.31. Bridle joint, used where a wide piece is being jointed into a thinner piece

lower edge but it does not matter whether the top haunch is square or sloping.

In work such as small tables and plinths it is often the case that a wide piece of wood has to be jointed to a narrower one.

Here the mortise and tenon joint would not be suitable and *Figure 8.31* shows a typical arrangement of the bridle joint, which is applicable to this situation. To minimise loss of strength the trenches need only be fairly shallow but the actual depth would depend on the sizes of the parts being jointed.

Box construction techniques

A wide variety of jointing methods is available for constructions of the box type. Actual choice depends on the nature of the job, amount of strength required and the importance of

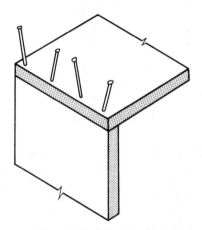

Figure 8.32. Dovetail-nailing

appearance, to name only three. All the joints shown are suit-able for solid wood, but those of an intricate nature, such as the comb joint or the dovetails, are not suitable for chipboard although, with care, they can be cut on plywood.

Figure 8.32 illustrates the simplest form of corner joint. The wood is merely butted together, with the strength coming very much from the nails employed. Ovals, roundheads and panel pins are all used for this purpose but it is usual to slope the nails as shown. This is known as dovetail-nailing and the arrangement resists being pulled apart more than it would if the nails were driven in straight. In any case, nails do not hold so well in end grain as they do in side grain so dovetailing is a good compromise.

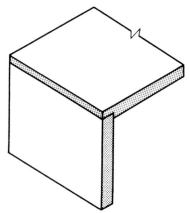

Figure 8.33. Rebated joint

The rebated joint in *Figure 8.33* is an improvement over the plain butt joint although it has little mechanical strength. The area that can be glued is slightly increased, but again the joint needs reinforcing with nails.

A form of tongue and groove joint is shown in *Figure 8.34*. It is wrong to make the tongue too long or too thick as this would result in a weakness between groove and the end of the wood, where splitting could occur because of the short-grain situation. Carefully cut and with a good adhesive, this joint will hold without nails or screws.

The finger or comb joint shown in *Figure 8.35* has the advantage of some mechanical strength, plus a wide area for gluing. It is a joint which is increasing in popularity, partly because it can be quickly cut with the aid of an attachment working in conjunction with a small circular saw, or with a power drill.

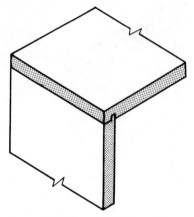

Figure 8.34. Tongue and groove joint

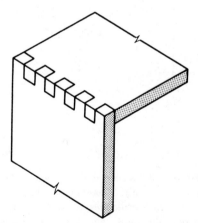

Figure 8.35. Finger or comb joint

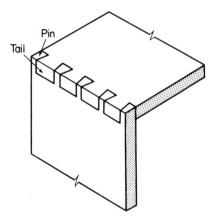

Figure 8.36. Common or box dovetail

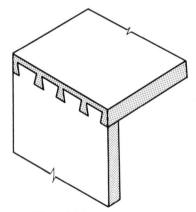

Figure 8.37. Lap dovetail

The common, or box dovetail, shown in *Figure 8.36,* is a strong joint that can only be assembled and pulled apart in one direction. The basic principles of the mating slope of pins and tails is that the joint cannot be pulled apart against the slope as, in fact, force applied in this direction makes the joint tighter. For this reason it is quite important on which member the pins should be cut. For instance, they should be made on the horizontal parts of a tool box which has to be carried, and on the front of a drawer. Such joints should always be glued.

In order to conceal the joint on one face, lap dovetails are used (*Figure 8.37*). This is the traditional joint for a drawer front and is sometimes referred to as a drawer-front dovetail. The piece with the lap is often thicker than the part with the tails.

Other dovetails which can be used for corners include the double lapped dovetail, where the joint is almost completely

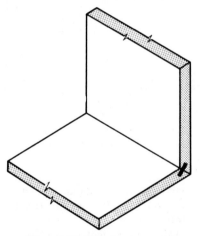

Figure 8.38. Mitred and tongued

hidden and the mitre dovetail, where the completed and assembled joint has the appearance of a plain mitre. Both require considerable skill to make properly.

A joint which is both neat and strong is shown in *Figure 8.38*, where the two members are mitred. For both maximum strength and appearance the tongue should have the grain running crossways, when the tongue becomes inconspicuous at the edges. This is a popular type of machine-made joint but can be tedious when made by hand.

The screw block method shown in *Figure 8.39* can be used on its own, or as a way of strengthening the methods shown in

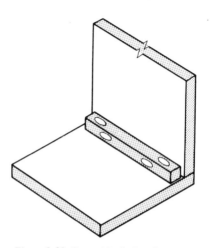

Figure 8.39. Screw blocked — slot-screws are not necessary with man-made boards

Figures 8.32 and *8.33.* As already mentioned, the screws must be slotted if the wood is solid, but this is not necessary with man-made boards.

There is a wide range of metal and plastics devices on the market nowadays, designed to simplify and speed up assembling construction of the type under discussion, especially in the commercial field. Many are of the K.D. (knock-down) type designed for furniture which can be packed flat in a carton and assembled at home. The most common of these is the corner block shown in *Figure 8.40.* It is a two-part fitting, each half being screwed to the respective pieces forming the joint, then the assembly is held together by a set screw joining the two half blocks.

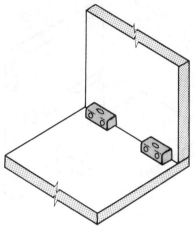

Figure 8.40. Modesty or corner blocks

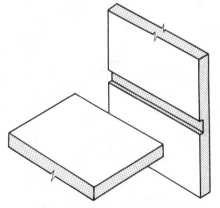

Figure 8.41. Through trenched joint

With many box constructions it is often required to have components which sub-divide the area formed by the four main sides. Through-trenching is a simple way of doing this and *Figure 8.41* shows the joint. Trenches of this nature are often made about one-third the thickness of the material.

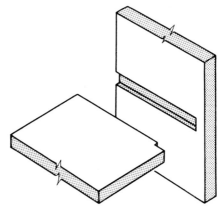

Figure 8.42. Stopped trench

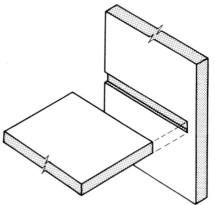

Figure 8.43. Stopped trench with division
fitting as far as the stop

In order to conceal the front of a trench when used, for instance, in a set of book shelves, a stopped trench as shown in *Figure 8.42* is often used. Frequently it is desired to have the edge of one piece deliberately not level with the other, as in *Figure 8.43*. The stopped trench is used. The double-stopped trench, as in *Figure 8.44*, is another variation of the joint.

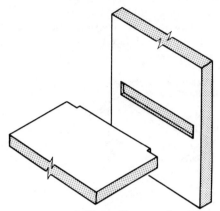

Figure 8.44. Double-stopped trench

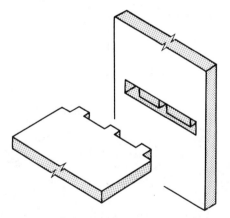

Figure 8.45. Combined trenching with mortise and tenons

Where maximum strength is needed the joint illustrated in *Figure 8.45* can be used. This is really a combination of a double-stopped trench with mortise and tenons. Details of the arrangement can vary considerably regarding number and position of the tenons, and whether the trench is double or single stopped. This joint is sometimes used as a decorative feature, with the option of inserting wedges of a contrasting colour to secure the tenons.

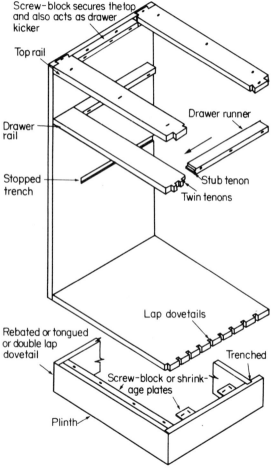

Figure 8.46. Construction of small cabinet, showing joints

The construction shown in *Figure 8.46* shows a small cabinet of the bedside type. This combines a great deal of joint applications and furniture-making practice. It can be regarded as typical of traditional techniques, but there are many alternatives depending, for instance, on appearance. For example, the top can be secured directly to the sides by rebating, tonguing or some form of dovetail, and the plinth can be of the integral pattern shown in *Figure 8.6*. Alternatively, small legs could be added to the underside.

Where the top is to be added separately to the main carcase, top rails are employed. The usual method of jointing these to the ends is by dovetailing. Note how the tails are off-centre: this is to prevent the corner of the carcase from being weakened and maybe splitting as a result. It is usual to add a screw through the joint. The back top rail is positioned to be level with the rebate. Screw blocks between the rails serve a double purpose and must be the same thickness as the rails. They act as part of the means of securing the top and also help to control the movement of the drawer. The kicker, which prevents the drawer from tipping when it is pulled out, must never be made a tight fit between rails because an allowance is needed in case of shrinkage.

The rail immediately below the drawer is called the drawer rail and the use of twin tenons is a way often used to joint the ends. Dowels can also be used as a quicker method. Tenons would normally be stopped.

Runners, which are the main components on which the drawer slides, are best if stub-tenoned into the back of the drawer rail. This joint is really for location purposes only, to ensure that the alignment necessary on the top surface for the smooth action of the drawer is achieved.

Cabinets of this nature often contain a shelf, and there are many ways of supporting such a part. For the more simple constructions the batten shown in *Figure 8.20* can be used, but trenching is a neater method. There are many fittings available for supporting the shelves. These are often used when there is a need to make the shelf adjustable for height.

A separate plinth is a common feature on small cabinets, and alternative ways of jointing the parts are available. In addition to the ones indicated on the drawing the tongued and mitred joint can be used at the front, and the rear part of the plinth positioned right at the back and jointed by rebating, tonguing or lap dovetails. Often on parts that are

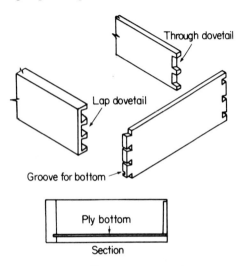

Figure 8.47. Drawer construction

completely out of sight, like the inside of a plinth, blocks are glued to the internal corners of the joints to add strength. These are known as 'glue blocks'.

The drawers illustrated in *Figure 8.47* indicate the time-honoured way of making a drawer, although again there are slight variations in how the bottom, nowadays invariably of plywood, is held in at the sides. Note how the dovetail on the front is lapped to conceal the joint, with the pins themselves arranged so as to resist the pull of the drawer. The back of the drawer is positioned to be level with the grooves in the sides, so that the bottom can be slid in after the sides are assembled.

This is seen in the sectional view. Not shown are the glue blocks usually added to the underside of a drawer. Glue blocks add a lot to the rigidity of a drawer and also increase the area on which the drawer slides.

Plywood is a very satisfactory material for the backs of cabinets. Two ways of adding this to the carcase are shown in *Figure 8.48*. A minor disadvantage of grooving (*b*) is that there

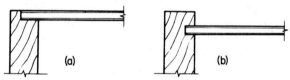

Figure 8.48. Fixing plywood backs to carcase: (a) rebated, (b) grooved

is a slight loss of internal depth. When rebated (*a*) fixing can be by glue, with pins or screws. Sometimes, to facilitate the finishing process, the back is not actually fixed until the finishing is completed. The back is then screwed or pinned in place.

Adhesives

We now have a great range of adhesives produced synthetically. Many of them are impervious to moisture, and some are boil-proof. Others bond on contact, after first being applied to both mating parts, others even bridge small gaps in jointing surfaces. These are called 'gap-filling' adhesives. The subject of adhesives alone is a big one but for general woodworking the many general purpose woodworking adhesives are suitable and makers provide full instructions. They are usually used cold; animal glues generally have to be heated, applied hot and the assembly must be cramped up before the glue cools.

There are some points to be considered when using glues and adhesives: wood is much stronger with the grain than across it, it varies in cell structure and moisture content. These things have an effect on the type of adhesive most suitable for the work.

Face grain to face grain or edge to face and edge to edge produces very strong bonds. End grain is, however, difficult because of the thousands of ends of hollow fibres that are involved. Adhesive must be applied generously to end grain and allowed to soak into the fibrous structure. Dowel joints are a big help with end grain.

When clamping glue joints together while setting the pressure should be firm enough to hold the parts close but not so firmly that all the glue is squeezed out of the joint. Any that does should be mopped away while still wet.

9 Wood Turning

Basic theory

Woodturning is one aspect of woodworking which is now exceedingly popular as a hobby, source of supplementary income or full-time occupation. There is a large range of wood-turning lathes on the market, from tiny machines for modellers to huge ones on which really large work can be performed. In between these extremes there are many makes of the most popular size for serious work — 762 mm (30 in) between centres. Such a machine will accept work up to 762 mm in length, which is long enough for table legs.

In Chapter 6 reference was made to drill powered lathes. They are limited in capacity and capability but they can produce many useful but smaller examples of the turners' craft, and can provide a good jumping off point for any one anxious to try out or develop his skills at turning.

There are also reasonably priced universal woodworking machines which include a lathe. With a much greater capacity than the drill-powered lathe, they also provide other operations such as band or circular sawing, planing and slot mortising. Some are basically a lathe, with the other operations carried out by attachments which can be added as the need arises. They are a sound investment for the keen woodworker.

Another term which relates to the size of a lathe is referred to as the swing. This is the distance from the lathe bed to the centres, which determines the maximum diameter that can be turned on the right-hand side of the headstock (see *Figure 9.1*).

A lathe with a 102 mm (4 in) swing will turn work up to a maximum diameter of 203 mm (8 in). Thus the term 'swing' indicates the maximum radius of work.

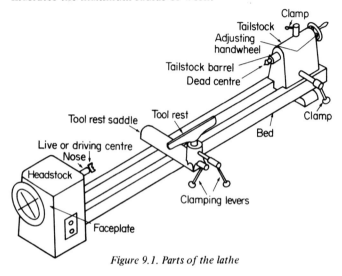

Figure 9.1. Parts of the lathe

Many lathes, however, are designed and equipped so that faceplate turning can be carried out on the left-hand side of the headstock, a facility known as 'rear turning'. Because there are no restrictions imposed by the lathe bed the diameter of work which can be done with rear turning is up to three times the diameter possible on the right-hand side.

Basic principles

If a block of wood is held horizontally between points on which it can be made to revolve it is possible to hold chisel-type tools, on a suitable rest, against the wood and gradually shape it in the form of a cylinder with parallel sides, or cut to give an elaborate profile. Similarly, if a block of wood is fixed to a revolving plate the tools can be used to hollow out and shape the block to make a bowl, platter, vase, table lamp and so on.

The lathe (*Figure 9.1*) has a headstock in which revolves the spindle. Almost invariably the machine is powered by an electric motor. Usually there are stepped pulleys on both spindle and motor which enable different speeds to be provided as the drive-belt is re-positioned on the pulleys. Speeds usually range from around 750 r.p.m. for large diameter work to 3,000 r.p.m. for work of small diameter.

When wood is being turned it is really the speed of the wood at its periphery which is important, rather than its r.p.m., i.e. the feet per minute speed of the wood as it passes the cutting tool. Too high a speed should be avoided, as this will result in dust being removed rather than shavings, which should be the aim. Ideal speeds cannot be achieved, especially for faceplate work. If, for example, a fairly large bowl is being turned, then the speed at which the wood passes the tool at the rim of the bowl is very much greater, for a given r.p.m., than the speed at which the wood passes the tool near the centre of the bowl.

For turning between centres, or spindle turning, a device called a live centre is placed into the hollow spindle in the headstock. This live centre grips one end of the wood. The other end is held on a fixed point or dead centre, on which the wood revolves. The dead centre is held in the tailstock, which is a sliding fit on the base, or bed, of the lathe. The headstock is fixed to the bed. An adjustable tool rest is mounted on the bed. It can be moved along the bed and locked in any position within the maximum capacity of the machine.

The live centre, also known as the driving centre, can be removed from the spindle and a faceplate screwed onto the threaded nose of the spindle. On this can be fixed a wood block of roughly circular shape. The tool rest can be adjusted to allow for both the hollowing of the block, and exterior shaping.

When wood is mounted between the centres it has its grain parallel to the axis of rotation. This is known as spindle turning. When wood is mounted so that the grain is at right

angles to the axis of rotation it is referred to as faceplate turning. There are subtle differences in technique between the two,
especially with regard to tool sharpening and handling.

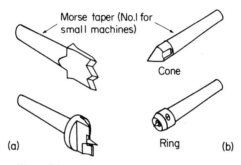

Figure 9.2. (a) Prong centres, (b) dead centres

Figure 9.2 shows different patterns of both driving and
dead centres. They have a tapered shank, known as a morse
taper. Tapers are number-graded according to their size. Most
lathes up to 762 mm (30 in) between centres size take a
number-one morse taper and the headstock spindle and
tailstock barrel are bored with a tapering hole to suit. The
mechanical principle of the morse taper is the circular wedge,
and even a small amount of end pressure creates adequate
friction for a positive grip between the two surfaces.

Work is also held on chucks, of which the most common
is the screw. Small screw chucks are mounted on morse
tapers but a better pattern is shown in *Figure 9.3*. This has a
fairly heavy gauge wood screw which is both renewable and
adjustable, so that the amount of projection can be varied.
Screw chucks of this type can be used for mounting wood
where the grain is parallel to the axis of turning, or at right
angles to it. Because the wood is held by a single screw its
capacity is limited, and this applies especially to the length
of a piece of wood when it is being held at its end. The greater
this projection the greater is the levering effect of the cutting
tool – the screw in end grain has limited holding power.

Other types of chuck include collet chucks, one which incorporates a coil spring to grip the work and one, recently introduced, where it is claimed that the work piece can be held by one of six different methods.

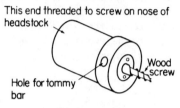

Figure 9.3. Screw centre

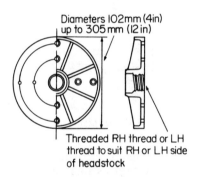

Figure 9.4. Faceplate

A typical faceplate is shown in *Figure 9.4*. This type of faceplate is drilled for screw, the usual way of mounting work on a faceplate. Different handed threads are used at the centre of such faceplates according to which side of the headstock they are to be used: standard clockwise thread for right-hand side of the headstock and anti-clockwise thread for left, or out-board side.

Engineers' type dividers or the more traditional wood-workers' wing compasses are used frequently before and

during actual turning operations. Prior to mounting a block
for faceplate work it should be cut approximately to circular
shape to eliminate projecting corners and reduce vibration
during preliminary turning. The wing compasses are a convenient means of marking out for this. During turning they are
used to scribe out circles indicating where cuts are to be made.
The compasses are set to the required diameter, one leg is
placed on the centre of the revolving work, and the other lightly
trailed against the work in order to scribe the working line.

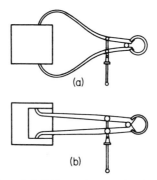

Figure 9.5. Calipers: (a) outside, (b) inside

Outside calipers are used far more than inside ones but both
have their place in the turner's tool kit. They are shown in
Figure 9.5. Simpler patterns of calipers are available without
the screw adjustment. Lateral marks, required on a piece of
wood during turning to indicate shoulders, steps, sinkings and
similar features, are done by pencil, the marks being transferred
directly from the rule to the work while it is revolving.

Tools

Tools used by the turner are relatively few but they are made
in many sizes and weights. For the drill-powered lathe small
tools are available and for larger machines tools called 'long-
and-strong' are quite popular. The principal tool is the gouge.

This is sharpened in a number of different ways according to the type of work it has to perform.

For the initial shaping in spindle turning a fairly large gouge of about 32 mm ($1\frac{1}{4}$ in) should be used. This is sharpened with its end square. Although all turning tools need grinding from time to time it is not usual to have a second bevel in the

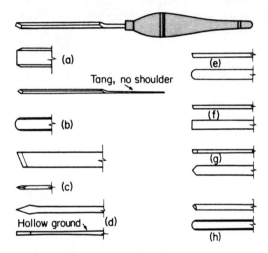

Figure 9.6. Turning tools: (a) square-ended gouge, (b) round-ended gouge, (c) skew chisel, (d) parting tool, (e) round-nose scraper, (f) square-nose scraper, (g) diamond-nose scraper, (h) gouge sharpened for faceplate work

same way that bench chisels and planes have. A typical turning gouge is shown in *Figure 9.6 (a)*, while at *(b)* is shown one sharpened with its end rounded. This type of sharpening is required on a gouge for concave shaping on spindle work.

The third manner of sharpening is shown at *(h)*. This gouge is prepared for faceplate work and has a bevel of 45 degrees. It can be steeper without loss of efficiency. Only relatively narrow gouges are used for faceplate work, rarely more than

13 mm ($\frac{1}{2}$ in). Patterns known as long-and-strong are popular for bowl turning, when 10 mm ($\frac{3}{8}$ in) is considered to be an ideal size. Many turners use gouges straight from the grindstone, and gain the cutting action from the burr so produced.

The parting tool, shown at (d), is included in all sets of turning tools and is in frequent use. It is used for squaring off ends, forming shoulders, and reducing diameters at specific points on the work. It is a very useful tool but it does not cut cleanly because of the nature of its cutting action. An end squared off with a parting tool would need attention from a skew chisel if the end of the work is to be seen.

A skew chisel (c) is used to make smoothing cuts for finishing and for cutting shoulders, beads, vees and convex curves. The exact angle at the end is not important but it is always policy to use as large a skew as possible, depending on the nature of the work. The heel of the chisel is used to bite into the work and the toe must trail, allowing the waste to curl off in a thin shaving. This is because in use there is the ever present danger of the toe digging into the work. Therefore, the wider the chisel the further the toe is away from the wood.

Tools shown at (e), (f) and (g) are classed as scrapers because they scrape the wood rather than cut it. They are used more on faceplate work. The most common of the scrapers is the round nose, used for finishing hollowed out work where a gouge cannot operate. Scrapers are ground with a steep bevel and work best when used straight from the grindstone.

Cylinder or spindle turning

Spindle work can, and should, be carried out entirely with tools that cut the wood. Such tools are gouges and skews. When used properly both are capable of removing long, continuous shavings from the wood − to the delight of the turner and amazement of the onlooker. The ability to remove very long shavings does depend to some extent on the species of wood as some respond to this technique better than others. When the wood is properly cut with the gouge and skew the surface is usually left smooth, and does not require much sandpapering.

Using the gouge and skew correctly is a knack acquired by experience, and until the proper way of using these tools is mastered the beginner will in all probability resort to scraping. This is, undoubtedly, easier and safer but scraping does not cut the wood anything like so cleanly as the gouge and skew.

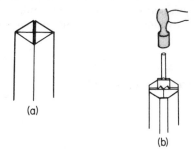

Figure 9.7. Preparing headstock end: (a) saw-cut in end, (b) prong centre tapped home

This has the result that the surface is left fairly rough, necessitating a lot of work with glasspaper. On long, slender work scraping can cause the wood to bow while revolving, as the wood will tend to resist the pressure and lower cutting efficiency of the scraper.

Stock to be turned between centres usually starts off by being square. Sufficient waste must be provided at each end for mounting and subsequent parting off. First the diagonals are drawn in at both ends, as in *Figure 9.7*. These locate the centres for mounting in the lathe. It helps if a diagonal at one end has a small V-cut sawn in it, as shown, and the centre of the other emphasised with a bradawl. It is also worth while, and saves time in the long run, if the corners are planed off the wood to reduce it to octagonal section. This lessens the work turning tools have to do, and also reduces vibration.

If the wood is rather hard, a pronged centre can be tapped home with a hammer, as shown. Live centre and wood are then returned to the headstock, and the tailstock positioned so that the dead centre engages in the small hole made by the bradawl at that end. The tailstock is then locked in the bed and the barrel is screwed up and tightened to drive the centre into the wood, then slackened off a little to permit free rotation. A spot of oil at the tailstock end reduces friction and prevents the possibility of burning, but a rub from a candle is even better as it will not penetrate and discolour the wood.

Figure 9.8. Position of gouge on work

Gouge pointed slightly in direction of movement

Figure 9.9. The gouge is pointed slightly in the direction of movement

The tool rest is now adjusted to within 3 mm ($\frac{1}{8}$ in) of the wood, and about the same distance above its centre. As a precaution, the work should be revolved by hand to ensure it does not touch the tool rest.

Tools should be held firmly with the left hand near the end of the blade, fingers gripping the tool and palm of the hand partly on the tool rest so as to control lateral movement. The right hand is used to control the handle; that is, to provide: the angle of tool to the work, as seen from the side in *Figure 9.8*; the angle of the tool to the work in plan, as shown in *Figure 9.9*; and rotational twist to the tool to determine actual cut.

Note that the tool is placed fairly high on the wood (*Figure 9.10*), the aim being to have the bevel rubbing the surface so that it forms a tangent to the cylinder. The tool should also be pointed slightly in the direction of cutting.

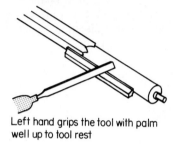

Figure 9.10. Left hand grips the tool with palm well up to tool rest

Left hand grips the tool with palm well up to tool rest

Figure 9.11. Using a skew chisel to smooth the surface

First stage of the cutting is with a fairly large gouge; this procedure is known as 'roughing down'. It matters little whether the cutting is from right to left or left to right but it will probably be necessary to move the tool rest as roughing down continues. The work should be checked frequently with calipers, set to a little more than the required diameter. It is safer to stop the machine when calipers are being used.

Smoothing a cylinder, and arriving at final diameter, is done with a large skew. *Figure 9.11* shows its position on the wood. It is placed high on the cylinder and positioned so that the centre part of the cutting edge is in contact with the surface. The handle is then lifted and rotated to enter the heel of the cutting edge to the depth of cut required, after which the tool is moved along the work. The skew is held in a similar manner to the gouge and, also like the gouge, it is better to move off at the ends, rather than on to the work.

The bevel of the skew acts as a fulcrum and the handle hand controls the actual cut. Point of contact with the work should be at the approximate centre of the cutting edge, or slightly nearer the heel. If a point too near the toe is used, the wood has a habit of taking control over the chisel, the toe digs into the wood and a piece is split out. Cutting can be carried out in either direction, the chisel merely being turned over.

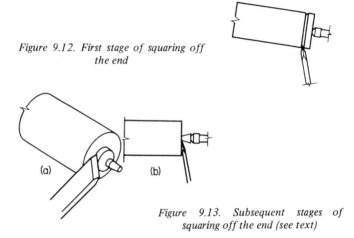

Figure 9.12. First stage of squaring off the end

Figure 9.13. Subsequent stages of squaring off the end (see text)

To square off an end, either the parting tool or skew chisel can be used. With the skew, a light nicking cut is made with the toe of the chisel, pushing the point directly into the work a trifle outside the required dimension, as shown in *Figure 9.12*. This cut cannot be made very deep so the chisel is now placed flatways on the wood, and pushed forward and downward at the same time. *Figure 9.13 (a)* shows this cut being made. To finish off the cut exactly to the line the chisel must be held as shown in (*b*). The essential point here is that the bevel of the skew adjacent to the end being cut must be nearly parallel to this end surface. There should be just a fractional variation from this plane, only enough to allow the toe to cut.

As an alternative to the skew, a parting tool can be used to square off an end in a similar way to that shown in *Figure 9.14 (a)* for forming a shoulder. For a shoulder with a tenon or a pin, the parting tool is used close to the shoulder line, and a

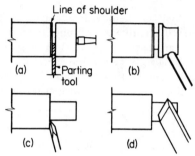

Figure 9.14. Stages in forming a pin, or tenon, at the end (see text)

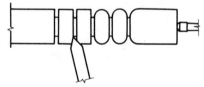

Figure 9.15. Beads formed with a scraping tool

cut made to within about 1.5 mm ($\frac{1}{16}$ in) of the required diameter. Waste is then removed with the gouge, as at (*b*). Next, the shoulder is trimmed back to the line with the skew, held as described for squaring an end, and as shown at (*c*).

The horizontal cut is also made with a skew. This is seen at (*d*) and only very light cuts should be taken, with frequent checks using calipers. Such a pin, or dowel, is often intended to fit into a hole so it is therefore wise to check it in a sample hole bored in a piece of waste wood.

Small beads are made with a convex cut and *Figure 9.15* shows a simplified way of forming the beads. Their locations

are pencilled in and the parting tool is used to form grooves
between the beads. Depths of the grooves should be made
equal, about half the width of the bead, and checked with
calipers. A diamond point scraper is then used to form the
profiles.

Scrapers are initially held horizontally on the tool rest, and
the handle moved slightly upwards until the tool is cutting the
wood rather than just rubbing it. The edge of the scraper
should be on, or slightly below, the centre line. If little more
than dust is being removed the tool probably needs sharpening,
but scrapers will never remove shavings as do cutting tools.

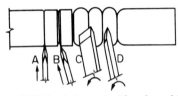

Figure 9.16. Beads formed with a skew chisel

Figure 9.16 shows a more professional approach to cutting
beads and is carried out entirely with the skew. The point, or
toe, of the skew is thrust into the work as at A. This incision is
enlarged to form a Vee by making the following cuts first at
one side, then the other, of the Vee, as shown at B. Depth of
cut is increased a little as subsequent rounding is carried out.
This must be done carefully in order not to sever the grain as,
otherwise, there may be a tendency for some slight surface
splitting along the grain. Actual rounding is done from the
centre of the bead downwards into the Vee, as in C. This
involves quite a compound movement of the tool, controlled
from the handle.

The chisel does not move laterally along the tool rest but,
for the left-hand side of the bead, the handle moves to the
right and is raised so that the cutting edge is lowered around
the curve of the bead, and at the same time the tool is rotated
slightly so that as it completes the cut the flat surface of the
chisel is almost upright, as at D.

As with the bead, alternative ways of forming a cove, or concave cut, are practised: one by scraping, the other by cutting with a gouge. For the more simple method of scraping a round nose scraping tool is used and the method of working is shown in *Figure 9.17*. It is always better to use a scraper that is smaller than the size of the hollow required, and the tool is moved in the manner shown.

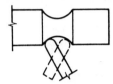

Figure 9.17. Cove or concave cut made with a round-nose scraper

Forming a cove with the gouge involves rather more skill when compared with scraping, but has the advantage that, when correctly executed, the surface is left very much smoother. This is because, with a sharp gouge, the wood is cleanly cut and with no tendency for the grain fibres to be torn out of the surface, which is always a possibility with scraping methods.

To cut a cove with the gouge, start in the centre part with the tool on its edge as shown in *Figure 9.18*. As the gouge is

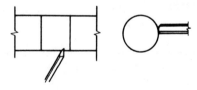

Figure 9.18. Start of cove or concave cut using a gouge

moved forwards, the right hand moves to the right while the left hand rolls the gouge over onto its curved back. This cuts the right-hand side of the cove. The action is reversed for the other side. *Figure 9.19 (a)* shows the cut well advanced, the gouge always working from the periphery downwards into the

hollow, and the turner always starting the cut with the gouge
well over on its side. The position of the gouge at the end of
the cut is seen at (b).

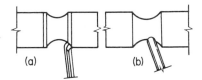

Figure 9.19. Forming a concave cut
(see text)

For maximum control the bevel of the tool must always
be rubbing on the work. This also produces the most efficient
cutting, and therefore the cleanest surface. Approaching the
work with the gouge pointing towards the axis of the wood
can be compared to using a plane with a vertical blade. The
plane would scrape the wood, not cut it, and a gouge used in
this manner is reduced to carrying out the inferior action of
a scraper.

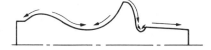

Figure 9.20. Direction of working on
compound shape

Most turning work involves curved profiles and as these are
either convex or a combination of convex and concave, a lot
of woodturning is based on the two fundamental cuts of
beads and coves, although the degree of curvature might be
much different. *Figure 9.20* shows the sort of combinations of
curves which may be found on typical turned parts. The
arrows indicate the direction of working, the rule being to
work from the large diameter to the smaller one whenever this
is possible. Hollow curves must be cut with a gouge or round-
nose scraper while convex curves and flat surfaces are formed
with the chisel, or square scraper.

Hollowed or faceplate turning

Faceplate turning has an inherent problem associated with it in connection with grain direction. This trouble is at the edge of the turning rather than the face. Reference to *Figure 9.21* shows the nature of the difficulty. Because of the combination of grain direction and rotation of the wood, two opposite

Figure 9.21. The problem of working against the grain with faceplate turning

quarters are inevitably cut against the grain. There are techniques to minimise the effects but the problem cannot be eliminated. When a piece of faceplate turning such as a bowl is examined it will invariably be found to have two areas opposite one another which are darker than the rest. This is because they are cut across the grain, exposing open pores which are more absorbent of light, reflect less, absorb more polish and so on, and are of a different general structure to the smoother, more reflective parts cut with the grain. This does, however, add to the character of good turnery and highly decorative wood.

Many turners prefer to have a piece of plywood sandwiched between the work and faceplate, and this is really essential when the wood being turned is smaller than the faceplate. In practice the ply is fixed to the work, then both pieces are screwed to the faceplate. Small screws may be used to fix the ply to the block but it can be brushed with a white resin type glue then covered with a piece of thick, rather soft, paper. The paper is then similarly glued to the block and the whole allowed to dry. The plywood is, of course, screwed to the faceplate. When the work is finished the ply and turned article are parted quite easily with a sharp chisel, and remains of paper and glue are washed or sanded off.

Figure 9.22 shows the use of ply packing, where the wood being turned is an ashtray. A recess is formed in the centre in order to take a brass or glass dish. For this the diameter of the sinking is marked out with compasses or dividers.

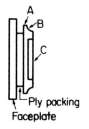

Figure 9.22. Section of simple faceplate work, such as an ashtray

It is usual to commence a piece of faceplate turning by truing up the edges to produce a disc of the required diameter, or a little larger to allow for further shaping, as at A in *Figure 9.22*. This can be done with the scraper or, more properly, with the gouge. The gouge is used well over on its side and pointing upwards so that the bevel is tangential to the surface.

Figure 9.23. Scraping tool sharpened on end and also partly at the side

This operation is best done by working from the flat surfaces towards the centre, so eliminating the chances of slight splitting at edges.

A square-end scraper is used for forming the recess indicated at C. This tool, however, needs 'relieving' on the grindstone on the left-hand edge, near the end. This is shown in *Figure 9.23*. There are two reasons for this: without the edge the scraper will not clear properly when cutting the outer edge of the sinking; the smaller the diameter of the recess the greater the need for this edge grinding. The second reason for the edge treatment of the scraper is that it creates a sharp edge, therefore the recess can be enlarged by moving the tool sideways and allowing the edge of the tool to do the cutting (*Figure 9.24*).

The edge of the ashtray can be shaped in a number of ways; the design shown at B in *Figure 9.22* can be formed with either a round-nose scraper or a small gouge.

Figure 9.24. Face of ashtray showing initial groove to form a recess, and the need to have left-hand side of scraper ground at an angle

One faceplate job which is always a favourite is a bowl. Bowls can vary considerably in shape but those shown in the illustrations are fairly typical. After mounting on the face-plate, shaping is commenced by using a square-nose scraper to form a recess as at A in *Figure 9.25*. This is made about 3 mm ($^1/_8$ in) deep or slightly more, after which the surface B is

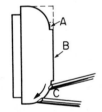

Figure 9.25. Early stage of turning a small bowl. Note that the bevel of the gouge is rubbing on the work, and that the gouge is fairly high on the surface of the wood (see text)

skimmed and also made very slightly concave. The curve to the lower part of the bowl is tackled next, preferably with a small gouge. The tool is kept over on its side and is pointed sideways and upwards so that the bevel is kept rubbing on the surface. This is illustrated at C, which also shows the movement of the gouge.

With the outside shaping completed, the bowl is reversed on the faceplate, making sure that it is concentric. Lengths of screws being used have to be watched carefully to make sure they do not penetrate into what will be the inside of the bowl.

The outside is completed with the gouge so that the curve blends in with the initial shaping. A gouge is preferred for the hollowing out process, or at least for the bulk of it. As hollowing progresses the tool rest is moved as in *Figure 9.26,* so that

Figure 9.26. Work reversed on faceplate for hollowing. Wood is removed using a round-nose tool, or a small gouge used largely on its edge. The tool rest is always kept close to the work

it is always only a short distance from the work. This is to reduce the overhang of the tool, and also explains why long-and-strong gouges are recommended for this type of work.

Depending on the exact shape of the bowl, it is sometimes difficult for even the experienced turner to make proper use of the gouge at the bottom of the bowl, near the sides. Here a

Figure 9.27. Completing the hollowing with a round-nose scraper

scraper often has to be employed. *Figure 9.27* shows this area of difficulty, with the tool rest once again adjusted so as to be fairly close to the work.

Finishing processes

Turned work, like most other woodworking projects, has to be glasspapered in order to prepare it for polishing or other type of finish. Before glasspapering, or sanding as it is more often called, the tool rest should be removed from the lathe bed.

Sanding is done with the work revolving, but fingers can be trapped if the tool rest is in position.

The glasspaper is held under the rotating work so that the frictional pull is away from the worker; if held the other way a sudden snatch from the work could break finger nails, or fingers. Medium pressure is applied and the glasspaper is moved slowly along the wood. In the case of spindle turning, too rapid a lateral movement could result in spiral scratches appearing on the work, as this sanding is across the grain. Progressively finer grades of paper are used until a smooth, scratch-free surface is produced.

Polishing is also done on the lathe. A simple way of polishing is by waxing. However, as in the case of cabinet work, it is helpful to give a sealing coat of french polish first and allow this to dry. Do not overlook the fact that this polish will have the effect of darkening the wood, so for light woods use white or very pale polish. Button polish gives a nice glow to darker woods.

Canauba wax is popular with turners. This is a very hard wax which is held, in block form, under some pressure against the rotating work. Frictional heat melts the wax surface and the wax sinks in and coats the work face. This is then burnished with a soft cloth, the lathe rotating at a slowish speed, until the polish is achieved.

Plastic type lacquers are useful for turned work as the effort in rubbing down and the burnishing required are done by the lathe itself. It is not too difficult with plastic lacquers to obtain an extremely high-gloss finish which is hard-wearing and resistant to most domestic hazards. If a tough finish without the gloss is required then fine wire wool, dipped in wax polish and held against the revolving wood, will leave a satin-like surface.

Only the basic outline of woodturning has been covered in this section. Many turners create their own designs as they turn the work, while others follow printed designs or copy items. If you intend to copy, make a card templet and check the work with it as you go along; alternatively, special templet formers can be purchased from craft suppliers.

Index

184